★ THE ★

CLASSIC

★ THE ★

CLASSIC

HOW EVERETT CASE AND HIS TOURNAMENT BROUGHT BIG-TIME BASKETBALL TO THE SOUTH

BETHANY BRADSHER

Whitecaps Media
Houston

Whitecaps Media
Houston, Texas
whitecapsmedia.com

The Classic: How Everett Case and His Tournament Brought Big-Time Basketball to the South
© 2011 Bethany Bradsher
All rights reserved

Photo credits can be found in the colophon at the end of the book

ISBN-13: 978-0-9836825-2-3

Printed in the United States of America

Second printing

Bethany Bradsher may be contacted through the publisher

To Sid, whose love gives me courage

A tournament is like a banquet,
and every game is a feast.

Everett Case

Contents

Introduction

It was late, close to midnight, one December night in 1956. A thirteen-year-old boy named Tim Nicholls had feasted all day at the hulking arena called the William Neal Reynolds Coliseum—feasted on hot dogs, on barbecue served up in the Reynolds basement, and most of all on basketball.

Nicholls was worn out, but it was the good kind of tired that comes from overdosing on something you love. As a Christmas present, he had received a coveted book of tickets for the Dixie Basketball Classic, so he had spent his day in Raleigh on the North Carolina State University campus watching four games featuring his favorite team, North Carolina, the host team, N. C. State, local favorites Duke and Wake Forest, and visiting squads Iowa, West Virginia, Utah, and DePaul.

Nicholls had one of the best seats in the house for much of the action—he had befriended the woman who played the coliseum organ, and she let him sit on the bench when she wasn't entertaining the crowd during time-outs or between periods. The teams from the North Carolina colleges, known as the Big Four, had dominated that day in the Classic's opening round. They all easily dispatched their out-of-state opponents, and the next afternoon Tim would come back to see his Tar Heels take on Duke. But before he could return to the Coliseum, he needed to get some rest.

As most of the fans streamed away from Reynolds toward the parking lot or their homes nearby, Tim walked deeper into the darkness toward Alexander Hall, a men's dormitory in the center of campus. In his pocket he had a key to the outside door, and when he reached the building he opened the door quietly.

He snuck into the lobby on light feet and navigated the dark stairwell to a room on the third floor belonging to a friend from his hometown of Canton, North Carolina. When classes were in session, the place was loud and bustling with activity, but the Dixie Classic was held between Christmas and New Year's, when the campus was shuttered for the holiday break.

For three years Nicholls stayed in Alexander Hall during the three-day staging of the annual Dixie Classic. In that time, he never turned on a single light. He crawled into bed each night, woke up and showered using the natural light of the dawn, and walked over to Reynolds for another dose of basketball. He never saw another person in the building.

"I was not supposed to be there," said Nicholls, who in adulthood became a successful Raleigh attorney. "It was understood that if I got caught this guy might get kicked out of school. So I would go in, I would unlock the door and take my shoes off, and I would go up the steps, and the whole time I was in the dorm I never turned on a light. In the morning I would get up and go over to Reynolds."

Nicholls stayed in the gloomy dorm room twice by himself and once with a friend from his hometown. While he watched basketball, his mother would visit relatives in the nearby town of Wendell, and each year, the morning after the Dixie Classic final, she would pick him up in front of Alexander Hall and they would drive back home to Canton, in western North Carolina.

There were times, walking alone on the dark campus or washing up in a shower that felt like a cave, when Nicholls was a bit afraid. But when he checked his program for the day's Dixie Classic offerings, he knew that loneliness was a small price to pay for daily access to the greatest holiday basketball tournament ever staged.

The Dixie Classic was created in 1949 by Everett Case, the head coach at North Carolina State and a basketball innovator of the highest order. Case instituted a host of new traditions and schemes for State's team, known as the Wolfpack, and his vision for hoops supremacy in the region is widely credited with moving college basketball from the background of the North Carolina sports scene to the place of honor it has occupied for decades.

Case dreamed big and expected greatness, and the flashiest symbol of that dream was the Dixie Classic, a three-day, eight-team spectacle that fast became the hottest ticket in sports if you lived in North Carolina and you followed teams called Wolfpack, Tar Heels, Blue Devils, or Demon Deacons. He had plenty of help from able administrators and skilled athletes, but from 1949 to 1960 Case boldly crafted an event so exceptional that its 1961 cancellation was still eliciting grief from fans fifty years later.

Before Everett Case came to Raleigh and the Dixie Classic became the stocking stuffer that every young fan dreamed of on Christmas Eve, basketball backboards in North Carolina driveways were scarce. World War II was still vivid, and the sport that had captivated the region in the prewar days was football. Case, reared in the refined hoops culture of Indiana, was the catalyst that upended that arrangement and made basketball king. His name has been forgotten by most of today's Big Four adherents, but his legacy is felt on all four campuses, where basketball dominance isn't just a wish, it's an expectation.

Consider the accomplishments of the North Carolina, N. C. State, Duke, and Wake Forest squads since the Dixie Classic was suddenly and unceremoniously shut down amidst scandal in 1961. In the decades since the tournament ended, Big Four teams have won the national title more than twenty percent of the time. At least one team from the Big Four made the NCAA Final Four thirty-two times in that half century, or sixty-four percent of the time. And the Big Four has produced ninety All-Americans in those years.

Those numbers are helpful in explaining modern-day phenomena like Krzyzewskiville, a tent city named after Coach Mike Krzyzewski which springs up each winter on the campus of Duke University so that students can camp out for prime basketball tickets. Some residents of "Kville," which is governed by student monitors and equipped with wireless internet service, stay in their tents for more than two months. Another fingerprint of Case's legacy is the Carolina Basketball Museum in Chapel Hill, an 8,000 square-foot monument to Tar Heel excellence that is the sole basketball-only museum on a university campus in the country.

In Raleigh, the very epicenter of Case's glory days, the teams fell on hard times after the last national championship in 1983, but a series of four different head coaches in twenty years demonstrates the school's determination to bring the shine back to the program that Case built. Modern Wolfpack fans share that yearning, as evidenced by a Facebook group created in 2008 called "Bring Back the Dixie Classic Basketball Tournament."

From a thirteen-year-old fan staying all by himself in a deserted dormitory to a community of fans willing to sleep in tents for weeks to procure a basketball ticket, extreme faithfulness to basketball in the state of North Carolina follows a clear road back to the Dixie Classic. It was a tournament that gave preeminence to the game and its fans, and its success has led to countless moments of glory on the hardwood, flashes of basketball sublimity burned in the memories of fans—fans who never knew that they owed a debt to a holiday tournament dreamed up by a coach and a sportswriter looking to fill a grand new arena and change the culture of an entire state.

I
EMERGENCE
1949–1953

One

In 1946 Everett Case had just finished serving his country in wartime—by coaching basketball. It was the thing he did best, as proved by the four high school championships he won leading teams in Indiana over twenty-three years. As a coach in the United States Navy, Case had caught the eye of a basketball coach and promoter named Chuck Taylor, who sponsored clinics and camps and would later lend his name to an iconic Converse shoe.

Case stood only five feet nine inches tall and had never played basketball past high school, but his reputation was solid in Indiana and throughout the U.S. service leagues, where he amassed a 56–5 record in two seasons. Taylor was impressed, and he was ready with an answer when two top North Carolina State University athletics officials asked him if he had any candidates for the coaching vacancy at N.C. State. Armed with Taylor's assurance that Case was the best coach in the country, the N.C. State trustees hired him before Case had ever set foot on the campus in Raleigh.

The new coach followed Bob Warren, who had been paid just $2,000 a year—and that from concession profits—and was granted no scholarships for his players. With the war behind them and intercollegiate athletics emerging as a peacetime priority, the N.C. State administrators assured Case that he would have the funds he needed to pursue excellence. They also showed him a hulking, unfinished building that went further to assure him of basketball's bright future at NCSU than any scholarship budget ever could.

It was little more than a framework of steel girders, but Everett Case knew in its early phases that Reynolds Coliseum would prove to be the most valuable partner he had en route to his goal of national prominence. Construction on the building had started in 1942, but the nation's increased involvement in World War II had forced contractors to stop the work after the foundation and steel support system were installed. When the war ended, capital priorities turned to new dormitories and classrooms, and when Case moved into his office in 1946 the steel grid that would become his coliseum had been untouched for three years.

Case's enthusiasm for the project, as well as the quick success he brought to N. C. State basketball, helped rekindle plans for the building, and in 1948 crews went back to work at the site on central campus. But the arena wasn't constructed exactly as planned. Soon after he took the new job, Case gave his opinion about the space, which was designed as an exact replica of the 9,000-seat Indoor Stadium on the Duke University campus in nearby Durham.

Case had big dreams for his new university and the team that he had recruited largely from his home state of Indiana. Even before it had walls, Reynolds Coliseum was to Case a symbol of the greatness that could be. And when a man like Case had big dreams, he needed a sufficient place to house them. Reynolds, he said, was not going to be big enough for the crowds he expected to draw. At his request, the plans were altered in the only way possible—by expanding the two ends—and 3,400 new seats were added.

C. A. Dillon, who started announcing State basketball games before Reynolds was built and went on to be the regular announcer in the Coliseum for fifty years, said the skeleton of the Coliseum convinced Case that he had taken the right job. "When Case came in, he said, 'I want it bigger.' But they had already put the steel girders up, so they didn't have anywhere they could go except down. They couldn't go any higher."

When Case moved into his house in the Cameron Village area of Raleigh, no one knew he was putting down roots that would transform the way his new state viewed the sport of basketball. A lifelong bachelor, the forty-six-year-old Case became known as "The Old Gray Fox" for his neatly groomed gray hair. He loved to entertain fellow coaches and other friends in his home, which was tastefully decorated and kept neat by Laura Stevens, an old friend from Indiana whose two sons had played high school ball for Case in Indiana. Known within Case's inner circle as "Mamar," she came to North Carolina with Case to work as his housekeeper, which she did until her death in 1961. Case was also known for observing a faithful nap time every day after lunch, scheduling speaking engagements and travel early or late in the day so that his daily rest would be undisturbed.

As he kept his eye on the building that would come to embody his legacy, Case got to work making North Carolina State a national basketball phenomenon. All but one of the players on his first squad, which in those days was known as the Red Terrors, hailed from his home state of Indiana, and these "Hoosier Hotshots" went 26–5 and inaugurated the notion of holiday basketball. Accustomed to a busy December schedule in Indiana, Case found that the North Carolina schools did not generally schedule games before Christmas, so he put together his own six-game Midwestern tour for the team. They won all six games.

Christmas-season basketball wasn't the only innovation Case brought to his new home. He also introduced now-ubiquitous traditions like dimming the lights during pregame player introductions and cutting down the nets after a big win. He was known for inventive practice techniques and he had a flair for the dramatic—like the era when he had his players warm up for games wearing red capes. He is also credited with making hoops tactics like the fast-break offense and the pressing defense more pervasive in the Southeast. "He was a little dynamo," Norm Sloan, a member of Case's first team, told author Ron Morris in the early 1980s. "He just crackled with energy. There was nothing routine or average about anything he undertook."

As word of the Red Terrors' winning ways got out on campus and beyond, the team became a magnet for new fans. Case hadn't been in Raleigh very long before an incident occurred that proved two points definitively: college basketball could induce hysteria in North Carolina, and Reynolds Coliseum was more than a luxury.

It was February 25, 1947, in the heart of Case's first season, and N. C. State was hosting the University of North Carolina at Frank Thompson Gym, the 3,500-seat dinosaur that had lately been characterized by sellout crowds. It was already standing-room only an hour before tip-off when a frenzied group of ticketless fans broke down one of the front entrance doors. Eight policemen and ten firefighters responded to the scene and promptly called off the game. Just two days earlier, two Purdue students had been killed at a home game in West Lafeyette when the bleachers collapsed, so the N. C. State officers held firm despite the crowd chanting, "We want a ball game! We want a ball game!"

Harry Stewart, a legendary NCSU fan who would later serve as the president of both the Wolfpack Club and the Tip-Off Club, was at a Raleigh hospital that day with his wife and their new daughter, who had been born that morning. He kissed his family and got in the car to head to the basketball game, but he was stopped in his tracks by a radio report about the incident.

In March of 1947, Case capped off his inaugural season with the Wolfpack by leading his team to its first Southern Conference championship. Case led his champions to the net, where they climbed up and cut it down in celebration, sharing an Indiana high school tradition that was soon carried out after big victories all over the nation. In December of that year, the Red Terrors officially became known as the "Wolfpack," and in February of 1948 the final shipment of steel arrived in Raleigh, jump-starting construction on Reynolds Coliseum after five years of inactivity.

As implausible as it may seem in a state that has been known to grant school holidays during the Atlantic Coast Conference tournament, in the 1940s North Carolina was known as football country. Gridiron giants like Duke's Wallace Wade and North Carolina's Charlie "Choo Choo" Justice had helped set the region's focus firmly on football, with basketball merely an afterthought. But with his roots in Indiana, where basketball was the undisputed king, Case was determined to help shift the tide in Raleigh. He made it his avowed goal to see a basketball goal in the driveway of every child in the area, and he was even known to pay for hoops out of his own pocket on occasion. "It was virgin territory," he told a newspaper reporter near the end of his life. "I could picture what could be done here."

But perhaps nothing sparked Case's enthusiasm more than a tournament. He loved the atmosphere created by tournament basketball, the showmanship of the event and the feeling that any team could press through and go home with a towering trophy. It was a passion born in Indiana, where high school ball had no size divisions and the smallest schools could play for the state title and sometimes, like the 1954 Milan High School team that inspired the movie *Hoosiers*, write the ultimate Cinderella story. Case was fond of saying, "A tournament is like a banquet, and every game is a feast."

In 1949 the stage was set for something special in Raleigh. A tournament-crazy coach was capturing the hearts of Wolfpack fans and the loyalties of top recruits from New York, Indiana, and points beyond. A groundbreaking arena was going up right in the heart of campus. According to the book *On Tobacco*

Road, a fanciful conversation in Case's home one day was the spark that became the Dixie Classic. Along with Case, those present were assistant coach Butter Anderson, Raleigh *News and Observer* sports columnist Dick Herbert, Case's friend Jonas Fritch, and assistant athletic director Willis Casey.

"We were talking about the new coliseum, and I said, 'When they finish it, who's going to run it?'" Herbert told author Smith Barrier in 1983. "I said that if they would give it to me for one week when school was not in session, I'd run it for them for nothing for the year. Everett perked up and wanted to know, 'What would you do?'"

Herbert hatched a plan that day, with the input of the others, of a tournament that would pit the teams known as the Big Four—North Carolina State, the University of North Carolina, Wake Forest, and Duke—against four of the best teams from outside the state. Soon, Herbert recounted, the discussion turned to a name for the event: "Somebody wondered what we'd call it, and I said, 'Well, it's Dixie and in the South.' Then Butter added, "In Indiana it's the Indiana Classic.' Everybody said, 'That's it. The Dixie Classic."

The seats were not even installed yet, but already Reynolds Coliseum had a date with eight teams invited to inaugurate the tournament that would soon be vaunted as the best holiday competition in the country. Case got on the phone and invited Penn State, Rhode Island State, Georgia Tech, and West Virginia. Willis Casey was named the tournament director, and he quickly became consumed with the details of the huge event. And Herbert went back to his newspaper desk with the assurance that papers would sell like hotcakes during the traditionally dead news time between Christmas and New Year's because of his ambitious idea.

The men who watched the tournament's birth each played a role, but Case seemed conjoined with the Classic. He was the tournament's innovator, promoter, and engineer, creating a format that would crown a champion but also offered a full consolation bracket so that every team would have the chance to play three games. The NCAA did not impose a limit on the number of games a team could play in those years, and Case reasoned that since his tournament would be early in the season it would give coaches an opportunity to experiment and adjust their schemes within the loser's bracket, removed from the pressure of a trophy but in the presence of top-notch competition.

Case also handpicked the officials for the tournament, and it was widely believed that if the Old Gray Fox did not like the way an official called a Dixie Classic game then he would not be invited back the following year, a practice that fueled opposing coaches' frustration as the tournament grew and N. C. State's perceived home court advantage seemed to take hold.

Whether it was gifts for visiting coaches or innovative Dixie Classic-only rules—like the one allowing the team that was fouled in the final two minutes to choose between a free throw and a ball possession—Everett Case saw the Dixie Classic as a massive canvas just waiting for his particular brand of artistry. It helped that the coach was a master marketer—the Raleigh Chamber of Commerce once named him Salesman of the Year. Said Bob Kennel, who played briefly for Case: "The Dixie Classic, it was just Everett Case, ahead of everybody and everything."

"It was a big deal," said Vic Bubas, who played for Case in the late forties and went on to become an assistant coach under Case and then the head coach at Duke. "He let it be known that we were starting something new and it could build. We knew we weren't going to blow the lid off in the first year. But we felt we were part of something special.

"I don't care what you call him: an inventor, a promoter, a visionary, a wonderful coach, a recruiter. He brought that whole package to this area and kicked it off in that way, and he's rightfully called the father of college basketball in this area."

As the first Dixie Classic inched into view, the tournament's architects had more than pairings and hotel rooms to think about. They needed a completed arena, and in late November contractors were still putting finishing touches on Reynolds Coliseum. The building finally opened on December 2, 1949, for N. C. State's season opener against Washington and Lee.

The Raleigh *News and Observer* called the $2.5 million structure "mammoth" and boasted that it was the largest building of its type south of Atlantic City, New Jersey. But even though basketball christened Reynolds and the Dixie Classic was soon to pack its seats, in its infancy the arena was viewed as a multipurpose building. In a *News and Observer* article about Reynolds on the day before it opened, the expected events were listed, with basketball games taking the ninth place: "It will be used for the annual 4-H Club Week, Farm and Home Week, graduation services, large agricultural and industrial meetings, the annual Future Farmers of America convention, livestock shows, farm machinery expositions, student dances, basketball games."

Reynolds certainly did host a variety of tenants in its lifetime, but in 1949 Everett Case, the man who single-handedly added 3,400 seats to the building, wasn't about to yield to livestock or farm machinery when his inaugural Dixie Classic opened on December 28. The West Virginia Mountaineers were the first to arrive, and Case greeted them warmly and showed them to their rooms at Raleigh's historic Sir Walter Raleigh Hotel. Georgia Tech, Rhode Island State, and Penn State would soon follow, with the latter two teams arriving in Raleigh by train.

Ticket sales had been promising for the inaugural event, but 1949 wasn't the sellout that would become *de rigueur* for the Dixie Classic. In fact, Wolfpack officials had enough uncertainty about local interest in the tournament that they enlisted the help of Walker Martin, a local businessman who agreed to buy five hundred tickets to help jump start the event. On the eve of the first game, according to the *News and Observer*, four thousand tickets were still available, and fans could purchase them for $1 each for an afternoon doubleheader or $2 each for the evening contests. A book of tickets, good for entry to all twelve games, went for $7.25 on the lower level or $4.50 on the upper deck.

Each of the tournament's three days followed the same schedule: two games in the afternoon, clear the arena, two games in the evening. The first day always pitted the Big Four teams against the four visiting squads, and the subsequent pairings matched winners against winners and losers against losers. More often than not, the second day would feature intriguing Big Four matchups since the North Carolina teams so often came out on top in the first round.

In 1949, Everett Case's Wolfpack entered the Dixie Classic 5–1 and as the hands-down tournament favorite. The home team's first-round opponent was Rhode Island State, a team that was garnering nationwide attention for a fast-paced offense that had given the Rams the highest scoring average in the nation for three consecutive years.

Case, fully aware of the bad publicity that could come from a loss in the first round of his flagship event, went to great lengths to drill his team for the fireworks Rhode Island State was sure to bring. In practice prior to the tournament, he added a sixth man to the second team during scrimmages, and also used two basketballs. The idea was to make his players adjust to defending players and balls that seemed to be everywhere, so that after six players and two balls the Rams' frenetic scheme might seem tame in comparison. It was the type of innovative preparation that southern basketball fans were coming to expect from the coach who had once written a master's thesis called, "An Analysis of the Effects of Various Factors on the Accuracy of Free Throws."

Of course, Case's teams demanded opposing coaches to do their homework, too. As word spread about his early N. C. State teams, high school players from around the state planned field trips to Raleigh to watch players like Sam Ranzino and Dick Dickey make one-handed jump shots—two-handed set shots were the rule in those years—and execute the fast break in an era of structured offensive sets. According to the program for the 1949 Dixie Classic, "State employs an intricate system, devised by Everett Case. It includes the fast break, post plays, center-in, center-out and the valuable pressing game. All of these types are used by the Wolfpack at whatever stage the State coach sees fit to utilize them."

Day One of the first Dixie Classic was Wednesday, December 28, and the first two competitors were Wake Forest and Georgia Tech, followed by the hyped N. C. State-Rhode Island matchup. After Georgia Tech topped the Demon Deacons, Case took the bench and, spurred by 33 points from star guard Ranzino, directed his Wolfpack to an 81–64 victory over the Rams. The crowds were catching on to Case's vision, and that afternoon 10,600 watched the doubleheader, setting a new record in the South for attendance at a daytime basketball session.

N. C. State dominated Georgia Tech 57–34 in the second round and went on to face Penn State in the December 30 final. The home team struggled to answer Penn State's zone defense in the early minutes, but NCSU adjusted at halftime and slowly pulled away. With a 50–40 decision over the Nittany Lions for the first Dixie Classic trophy, the Wolfpack asserted its dominance in the landscape of southern basketball and reminded the seven other teams that this was *their* backyard.

Senior Dick Dickey, the N. C. State captain, was named the first Dixie Classic Most Valuable Player, and the other three Big

Four teams went home with little eagerness for the next year's event. The Tar Heels, Demon Deacons, and Blue Devils made some money from the tournament—Case had formulated an agreement that gave each team one share of the gate proceeds and N. C. State two shares—but in the early years they looked like members of the court, propping up the Wolfpack royalty who intended to stay on the throne indefinitely.

As News and Observer columnist Dick Herbert penned after the first tournament ended, "One can't help but wonder about the size of the crowds that would attend the Classic if all of the Big Four members equaled the State Wolfpack in ability."

Even with the champion virtually a foregone conclusion, the attendance figures were mind-boggling in a city of 65,000 whose previous basketball arena held only 3,500 fans. A record crowd of 11,700 watched the final game between N. C. State and Penn State, bringing the three-day total to 54,300. From a conversation in his home with a few friends, Everett Case had built something that would captivate the nation's basketball fans and transform the city of Raleigh for three days between Christmas and New Year's.

"Above everything else that he did, this was his event, his showcase," said Tim Peeler, the de facto historian of Wolfpack sports. "He had the best basketball arena in the country, and the only reason the Dixie Classic was born was so that he could show it off. He knew that the best way to really promote was to have the best arena, bring teams in, and then beat the crap out of them. And that's exactly what he did."

Not very far outside the Raleigh city limits, enthusiasm for the Dixie Classic was considerably more muted. Richard Crowder, who played for Duke from 1950 to 1952, recalled when he and his teammates got the news from coach Hal Bradley that they would be spending part of what was formerly Christmas break playing a tournament. "All of the other students had gone home for a two- to three-week Christmas vacation; we stayed in the dormitory and the only people we saw were foreign students," Crowder said. "We felt so sorry for ourselves, really."

It was not much better at North Carolina or Wake Forest. The Tar Heels, under Coach Tom Scott, had compiled eighteen consecutive winning records and made it all the way to the NCAA Final Four in 1946, but they lost two out of three games in the first Dixie Classic, to West Virginia and Rhode Island State. Woollen Gym, the Tar Heels' home venue, had half the capacity of Reynolds Coliseum with only 6,000 seats, and the bleachers had to be pulled out for every game.

But despite the disparities between the teams, the early years of their participation in the Dixie Classic highlighted one of the most unique geographical trends in intercollegiate athletics. In 1949, no more than forty miles separated any two of the Big Four schools, and Reynolds Coliseum was an easy trip for each group of fans. Their proximity gave rise to the nickname Tobacco Road. Case's design of the tournament structure insured that no Tobacco Road schools would play each other on the first day, so a regional camaraderie was born, with rivals cheering for each other as a unified force during the run of the tournament.

Of course, the connections between the teams were not limited to shouts from the stands. There was also plenty of gloating and comparison, and the proximity of the rival campuses provided an enticing possibility. Murray Greason, Jr., whose father was the head coach at Wake Forest from 1933 to 1957, said, "If somebody beat one of the other Big Four, it was very easy to get four or five cars together and just drive over to the other community and ride around tooting your horn. The rivalry was very intense."

The inaugural Dixie Classic was certainly more exhilarating for the host school than for any of the visitors, but that first event gave players and fans alike a glimmer of the spectacle that would grow as the 1950s dawned. The Wolfpack continued to dominate in Reynolds Coliseum when the first visitor of the New Year—defending NIT champions San Francisco— came to town and met with a resounding 69–54 defeat. But in the homes and businesses of Raleigh and beyond, the year of sports seemed like a lead-up for that adrenaline rush that the Dixie Classic would bring just after Christmas.

Two

Any epic tale needs a compelling setting, and as Reynolds Coliseum's spanking-new seats became broken in and the arena developed its own personality, the building asserted itself as a main character in the Dixie Classic storyline. Some of Reynolds' distinctive features were part of every game played there and some were unique to the tournament, but Dixie Classic visitors, even half a century later, remembered the sights, sounds, and smells of the building with remarkable clarity.

The most vivid recollection of the Reynolds atmosphere, striking now in its utter contrast to today's sporting events, was the thick haze of smoke that attended every Dixie Classic game. In the fifties, in a state where tobacco was king, smoking was so ubiquitous that even the coaches were known to light up from time to time. Former N. C. State assistant coach Charlie Bryant said that the fans with upper-level seats actually had trouble identifying the players on the court after the first game or two, so thick was the haze in the air.

"It was like you were playing below a big cloud—all 12,400 people, smoking," Bryant said. "People smell a cigarette halfway down the block today and start screaming bloody murder. Back then everybody in the damn building was smoking, even the coaches on the bench. They used to have butt containers at the end of the bench."

Of course, even though Everett Case and his friends deserved the credit for birthing the Dixie Classic, it is likely that he would not have had the Big Four or his coveted arena if not for the profits that North Carolina tobacco companies were turning during those years. Two of the regular Dixie Classic competitors came from campuses that owed much of their existence to tobacco money, and the very arena that housed the tournament paid homage to a tobacco magnate. As one state legislator once boasted, "In North Carolina, tobacco is as sacred as a cow in India."

The American Tobacco Company, owned by James B. Duke and based in Durham, controlled ninety percent of the world tobacco market until deregulation broke its hold in 1911. In 1924 Duke established the Duke Endowment and awarded an astounding $19 million to a small Methodist school called Trinity College that had opened in Durham in 1892. Trinity used the money to build a new campus and changed its name to Duke University to honor its benefactor.

Just twenty miles east of Duke, Wake Forest University, a private Baptist school founded in 1834, was experiencing a post-World War II rebirth with the help of a variety of endowments. But the most influential gift came in the mid-1940s, when the Z. Smith Reynolds Foundation—a charity founded by executives of the R. J. Reynolds Tobacco Company in Winston-Salem—offered to give Wake Forest $350,000 a year in perpetuity on the condition that the entire campus be moved from Wake Forest, North Carolina, to Winston-Salem, one hundred miles west. The proposal was accepted, and Wake Forest officially relocated to its new home in 1956.

As those two private institutions were blossoming with the help of tobacco foundations, W. N. Reynolds, the chairman of the board of the company his brother R. J. Reynolds had founded, was becoming a familiar face at North Carolina State, where he made one large donation to faculty salaries in the forties and where his niece Mary, upon learning that the Reynolds family had made only small gifts to the new coliseum, gave $100,000 toward the building's completion and requested that the building be named for her influential uncle.

With such a storied relationship between the state's key universities and tobacco, the voluminous smoke that shrouded Dixie Classic games incited little reaction in the tournament's heyday. Fans in those days reserved their wonder for innovations like the coliseum's organ or its popular "noise meter."

The arena's Hammond organ, selected by Everett Case himself, was situated near the corner of the court on the first level (the spot prized by young teenager Tim Nicholls who was often offered the organist's extra chair). Several different organists were given the honor of playing during the twelve-year run of the Dixie Classic, and they played during player introductions, halftime, and time-outs. The frequent organ music was one of the Reynolds accoutrements that North Carolina coach Frank McGuire would later complain consti-tuted an unfair home court advantage for his rivals from N. C. State, complaining that the Wolfpack seemed to gain a ten-point edge every time the organist played "Dixie."

Assisting the organ in creating a unique ambiance, high in the Reynolds Coliseum rafters, was the legendary "noise me-ter," a vertical row of light bulbs suspended from the ceiling. Vic Bubas, who played in the first two Dixie Classics and then coached in the other ten, remembers when the simple device was constructed and installed, and at the time he was a little dubious about its potential to motivate fans.

As it turned out, that row of light bulbs had a powerful influence on the 12,400 people seated below it. The bulbs would light up, one at a time, as the fans upped their volume. Bucky Waters, who played for N. C. State in the early fifties, remembered the frenzy that would ensue when only the final red bulbs on the meter were still dark, prompting the crowd to collaborate on a deafening roar that would finally illuminate the last row of lights. But the meter, another piece of Case's marketing genius, was also an elaborate trick on the Reynolds Coliseum faithful. It was a Coliseum employee in the press area, with his finger on a set of manual switches, who decided when to light up the bulbs on the noise meter.

"These were intelligent people," Waters said. "And their eyes were bulging, and their veins were sticking out in their neck, and they were screaming, 'Wolfpack! Wolfpack!' And there's a guy there with his finger on the little dial. It wasn't high technology. It was a guy with his finger on a little gadget."

In quieter moments, during Dixie Classic halftimes, the Reynolds court offered a performance venue for a variety of acts from Raleigh and beyond. The halftime entertainment, booked by tournament director Willis Casey, ranged from singing groups to gymnastics and dance teams. The inaugural 1949 event featured a group from a small town south of Charlotte, according to the Raleigh *News and Observer*: "At the halftime of each game, special entertainment has been arranged. Today, for instance, the well-known Cramerton dance team, which shows why square dancing is so popular, will put on a brief show at the halftime of the Georgia Tech-Wake Forest game and at the intermission of the Duke-Penn State contest." Later that evening, the offerings included the "crack tumbling team" from the University of North Carolina and the Raleigh Choral Group, featuring a hundred voices.

As a young teenager in Greensboro, Dick Frank accompanied his dad on several father-son pilgrimages to Reynolds in the Classic's early years. For him, the sounds of the tournament included the music played by one of the visiting acts, the band from Central Prison in Raleigh. A music enthusiast, Frank was impressed by the band and leaned over to his dad one afternoon to tell him so. "I would say, 'That's a great band,'" Frank recalled, "and then my dad would say, 'Well, they oughta be good. They've had a lot of time to practice.'"

Tumbling and dance were not the only diversions for attendees who wished to supplement full-court presses and free throws with a bit of flash. For each tournament, a co-ed from one of the participating schools would be named the Dixie Classic Queen, earning herself a full-page photo in the event program as well as travel expenses, lodging, and a fresh corsage every day of the tournament. Her chief official duty involved handing out trophies after the championship game, including the award to the tournament's most valuable player. In 1950, Dixie Classic Queen Sarah French from Tulane University kissed N. C. State player Sammy Ranzino so passionately during the MVP presentation that Ranzino dropped his trophy, and the photo was disseminated in newspapers across the state.

Classic organizers searched diligently for the right young lady each year, and in a 1956 press release NCSU athletic staffer Harry James described the process that led to the selection of Marie Barlow, a University of Utah student whose figure, according to the release, measured 35-23-35. "We have finally been able to select our Dixie Classic Queen, and we are enclosing several pictures which we believe are indicative of the young lady's true appearance," James wrote. "We had 29 contestants, and the girl we picked was one whom we felt would be a fine representative, both from the standpoint of beauty and also due to the fact that she comes from a famous University of Utah basketball family."

Connie Pinyoun had just finished her first semester at Wake Forest when she was selected as the Queen of the 1958 Dixie Classic. It was an honor that meant more to Pinyoun than to most young women; she grew up in Raleigh and went to a number of Dixie Classics as a girl. Years later she still recalled her queenship fondly, even if she had become a little too exuberant when she was given the ball to toss up for the tip-off at the first game. "Because I so wanted to do it well, I threw the thing way up over the scoreboard, so they had to have the referee do it over," she said. "It was not my shining moment." Despite that one miscue, Pinyoun soaked up the experience. She watched every game that year from a guest box shared by North Carolina Governor Luther Hodges and posed for countless photos.

"How often do you have people wanting to take your picture?" Pinyoun said. "To be chosen to be a Dixie Classic Queen meant a lot, because I had gone to the Dixie Classic and I had always looked up to the Queen."

At the hub of every Dixie Classic detail, from the Queen selection to halftime bookings to the hiring of thirty extra custodians to clean all night between tournament days, was N. C. State assistant athletic director Willis Casey, who managed every Classic. Casey, who would serve as the university's athletic director from 1969 to 1986 and be considered one of the most effective administrators in the Wolfpack's history, was the one who did more than anyone else to make Everett Case's grandiose dream a spectacular reality. "He ran the show," said Bill Hensley, who handled media relations for the Dixie Classic for five years. "Willis was very energetic and vivacious and very intelligent. If I wanted anything done, I'd go to Willis."

"Everett was a marketing genius, everybody would tell you that," said Charlie Bryant. "And he was also very fortunate to have Willis Casey around to help him out. Willis probably had a lot more to do with the development of the Dixie Classic than has ever been chronicled. Those of us on the inside who knew what went on knew the genius of Willis Casey, the ideas that he came up with and the things he made happen."

As it turned out, the years he spent mired in the minutiae of the Dixie Classic seeded a vision in Casey that would later become the preeminent tournament in all of college athletics. As a member of the NCAA's college basketball committee in the late seventies, Casey and Big Ten Commissioner Wayne Duke were the two architects of the NCAA Basketball Tournament's expansion from sixteen to forty-eight teams in 1980. Among the innovations that Casey and Duke brought to the tournament structure were at-large bids, a seeding structure for each region, and the elimination of the rule that limited each conference to only one qualifying team.

Duke was named to the college basketball hall of fame for contributions that included his NCAA tournament restructuring, but he said that Casey was his full partner in the development of what is today an annual wave of hoops fanaticism known as March Madness. "I was the chairman of the NCAA tourney committee, and Willis was a committee member," Duke said. "We had more ideas alike than most people, whether good or bad. Willis and I were the ones who were behind the expansion of the tournament."

Details large and small can be traced to the hand of Casey. A native of Goldsboro, North Carolina, Casey went to his hometown for the fulfillment of the idea to sell barbecue in the basement of Reynolds Coliseum between sessions of the Dixie Classic. He asked the proprietor of Griffin's Barbecue if he wanted the job, and Griffin's became the only on-site dining option offered at the tournament. Wilber Shirley is best-known in eastern North Carolina as the owner of a decades-old Goldsboro institution called Wilber's Barbecue, but in the 1950s he was a young employee of Griffin's who made a perennial pilgrimage to Raleigh to serve the Dixie Classic faithful. Those were more than business trips for Shirley; they were the beginning of a lifelong passion for Wolfpack basketball.

"I was right young, and I had not paid too much attention to college basketball before that," Shirley said. "We would feed them between the evening and afternoon sessions, and then I would usually stay for the games. With 12,400 people in the Coliseum, you had a pretty good number who would come through. They didn't have a lot of time to go out and eat and get back. So a right many people came to eat." The standard offering in the Reynolds basement, he remembers, was a pork barbecue plate with cole slaw, potato salad, and hush puppies on the side.

The Coliseum's invitation to Griffin's Barbecue is surprising, since an early proposal to keep the N. C. State dining hall open for Classic fans was rejected because of opposition from Raleigh restaurant owners. Local businesses saw the Dixie Classic as a providential antidote for the post-Christmas retail slump, and even with barbecue plates right downstairs, a number of establishments near campus became the beneficiaries of the tournament's emergence.

Just down the street from the NCSU campus, a new shopping center—opened the same year as Reynolds Coliseum—was changing the way Raleigh residents did business. Cameron Village, the brainchild of developers J. W. York and R. A Bryan, celebrated its grand opening in 1949 with four stores and one restaurant. An open-air shopping center, Cameron Village was considered the first development of its kind between Washington, D. C., and Atlanta. And it was a favorite destination for Dixie Classic fans. Just a month after establishments like the Village Restaurant and the Cradle Shop welcomed their first customers, they greeted an influx of visitors who had come to town for the inaugural Dixie Classic.

Johnny Ballantine's father operated cafeterias in two different downtown locations, and in 1960 the family opened a three-story eatery—with cafeteria, sit-down restaurant, and banquet hall—in Cameron Village. Ballantine remembers wondering if they would have enough food to satisfy the endless stream of basketball fans coming through the doors. "We had more business than we could handle," said Ballantine, who estimated that they fed two thousand in the cafeteria and more than two hundred in the restaurant during the tournament's run. "We had a cafeteria with two serving lines, and we had a restaurant on the lower level, and we just were mobbed from Thursday through the tournament."

Men's clothing stores, like Nowell's in Cameron Village, Wright's Clothing, and Varsity Menswear on Hillsborough Street, ran large display ads in the local newspaper advertising Dixie Classic sales; and hotels like the Sir Walter Raleigh, which provided lodging for the visiting teams, also benefited from the Classic crowds. In a 1958 article in the Raleigh *News and Observer*, reporter David Murray crunched the numbers surrounding the Dixie Classic and calculated big profits for vendors both inside and outside the Coliseum. "The Dixie Classic fan—a vigorous sport with strong vocal cords plus a genuine appreciation for basketball talent—turns out to be one of Raleigh's most tangible assets," the article read. "When 12,400 people gather at the same place twice a day for three days, the dollar signs multiply like tears at a wedding."

Among Murray's findings: Classic attendees spent at least $110,000 a day in Raleigh during the tournament in the late fifties, twenty-five percent of the out-of-town fans paid for lodging and food for the three-day event and spent as much as $20 a day, and ticket gross receipts in 1957 totaled $113,432.50. Those gate proceeds were divided equally among the eight participating teams, with N. C. State receiving a double share as the tournament sponsor. In 1957, each of the competing teams took home $7,453.81—a sizable purse in an era where concession workers were paid just $7 a day—and N. C. State netted $14,907.60.

The tickets themselves were a steal by today's standards—between $1 and $2 a game when the tournament started—but as the Classic exploded in popularity tickets became valuable commodities, and those without ready access had to get creative. Speck Underwood was eleven years old when the Dixie Classic started in his hometown, and he was basketball-obsessed and determined to get a view of the court. He did not have a ticket, so he developed a habit of sitting on the Reynolds Coliseum steps right around the time that the afternoon session would be ending. He was looking for fans from the losing teams.

"I would see the parents and all of the people that had come from each place, they would just get so upset they would take all of their tickets and just hand them to me, because they had lost," Underwood said. "And I would end up with a big stack of tickets every single time. Then on Saturday, that's when I would sell them. I had to sell them for the cost of the ticket, but I got to go, and I made some money."

The best part of this entrepreneurial venture, Underwood said, was seeing the faces of the fans who had come from out of town, who were following their team to the Dixie Classic with high hopes that their boys would be the first ones to topple one of the Big Four teams. But in twelve years, a team from outside North Carolina never took home the trophy.

When Underwood was twelve or thirteen, his seat on the steps proved ineffective and he found himself without a ticket. Undeterred, he asked a coliseum employee if they needed any help selling concessions. They hired him to sell drinks in the stands, but in retrospect he might not have been the most attentive employee the event ever had. "I went over there and knocked on the door, and I said, 'I've got to do this,'" he remembered. "I was selling drinks, but I spilled half of them because I had to look at the game. And I had to keep up with that money, and I had to pass them down, and do it at the right time, and I didn't want to miss the game, and I didn't want to trip and spill all of them."

Local kids were not the only ones hatching creative schemes to get into the building *sans* tickets. As a Wolfpack football player, Ken Nye was hired to sell programs at the Classic. It was a gig that got him in the door, but some of his football teammates wanted to watch the action, too, so Nye and the others who got in first would sell programs for a while, then lower the money belt out the window to their friends waiting below, who would enter the gates under the guise of selling programs.

But the most unusual route into Reynolds had to be the one taken by the Wake Forest basketball players in the mid-fifties. Their assistant coach at the time was a North Carolina sports icon named Bones McKinney, a gregarious, memorable big man who had played in the NBA and took a position under Demon Deacons coach Murray Greason to earn extra money while he studied at the Southern Baptist seminary adjacent to the WFU campus. All of the players were given passes to attend the games they were not competing in, but McKinney saw those passes as a source of profit for the Wake Forest basketball program, so he collected them.

That would have left players like Jack Murdock out in the cold, if not for an ingenious solution. "Wake Forest didn't have a lot of money," said Murdock, who was a star guard for the Demon Deacons. "When we would go through the door to get into the arena, Coach Greason and Bones would take up our participant passes, so we had to wander around until it was time to play. We'd go to the back door, and I remember knocking on the laundry chute, and we'd all go through the laundry chute." The coliseum laundry chute ran from the back of the building to the basement. One by one, the team members slid down the chute, dusted off their clothes, and strolled into the arena to watch some basketball.

Wake Forest's laundry chute escapade was not the only evidence that college basketball players received less than star status in those days. Alley Hart played for WFU after Murdock, in the late fifties, but he and his teammates were almost sent packing when they were supposed to be in the arena warming up for a game. The players were in the team bus, waiting to go inside to warm up, and the Reynolds security staff told Bones

McKinney that no one would be admitted without a ticket, no exceptions.

Even if they were occasionally disregarded, most players still regarded the Dixie Classic as an event worthy of burning some Christmas vacation time. The North Carolina teams usually stayed at hotels near Raleigh to prepare for the Classic, and Case pulled his Wolfpack out of their dormitories so that they could unify and focus on the task at hand. Dickie Hemric, one of the great big men in Wake Forest history, remembered being struck by the size and intensity of the crowds streaming into the coliseum. "That was the grandfather of all," Hemric said. "That was really a spectacular, a county-fair like deal. They would take their vacation and come to the Dixie Classic."

Of course, the Big Four teams were expected fixtures at the tournament, but Case and Casey went above and beyond to make sure that the out-of-state teams were treated like dignitaries. Each of the visiting teams had an NCSU staffer assigned to them to take care of any requests they might have, and coaches and players even took home some swag. In 1952 each player was given a cravat bearing tiny tar heel footprints, in recognition of the host state's nickname. And in 1954, at a special luncheon organized by the NCSU Tip-Off Club, each coach was presented with a country-cured ham.

Those luncheons became highly anticipated gatherings, known more for bawdy humor and silly skits than for the occasional remarks about basketball. Harry Stewart, who served as president of both the Wolfpack Club and the Tip-Off Club during those years, was often the emcee of the luncheons, and he was always quick with a witticism. The Raleigh *News and Observer* was there to recount the meal's high points:

"Over the years these Tip-Off clambakes have developed into rich entertainment," read an article from December 28, 1954. "The couple hundred club members, athletic officials, newspaper and radio men who attend always come away with a good supply of jokes, but not exactly the kind you'd care to tell at a Sunday School picnic. Basketball coaches, for some reason or other—perhaps through much practice in making impassioned pleas to likely prospects—usually rank high in the oratorical league, and the Classic bunch proved to be no exception. They brought along a good store of yarns to exchange for the ham."

In a time when television was still a toy for the wealthy and the NCAA and NIT tournaments were restricted mostly to venues in the Northeast, the Dixie Classic was gaining a reputation as an entertainment destination of the first order. Vic Molodet, an Indiana boy recruited by Case who played for N. C. State in the mid-fifties, compared it to the horse races at Saratoga Springs. "It was more or less a happening," said Molodet. "It was the tournament of tournaments, there's no doubt about it." Only a year or two after its invention, the Dixie Classic was fast legitimizing the hyperbolic pronouncement made about it by the Raleigh newspaper before the first game had even been played: "The Dixie Classic, heralded as the South's greatest basketball tournament."

The hype was fed by many things: the noise meter, the organ, the teams flying in from thousands of miles away and going home with country hams. But if the Dixie Classic's popularity was going to be sustainable, it would have to happen not in the rafters or in the Cameron Village eateries, but on the basketball court. The Dixie Classic crowd would gladly soak up the atmosphere, but for most of them the purpose of the trip was to sit amid the smoke and focus on the games that made all of the rest possible.

Three

Everett Case might have been the only coach in America with enough vision to birth the Dixie Classic, and in the tournament's youth his teams seemed to be the only ones with enough talent to excel there. Case, his staff, the Wolfpack players and fans, and the city of Raleigh loved the new showcase for their squad, which was enjoying national rankings on a regular basis and attracting top players from Indiana, New York, and as far afield as Denver. N. C. State staked its particular claim on its home tournament by winning every one of its Classic games for four straight years and making sure that the first four trophies stayed right there in Raleigh. C. A. Dillon, the legendary Reynolds Coliseum announcer who called every Dixie Classic game, remembers that most of the early games were so dominated by the red and white that they were, from a basketball standpoint, boring.

"There wasn't anybody that came in there that we didn't send home," said Vic Molodet, who played for the Wolfpack in the mid-fifties. "We sent 'em home pretty good." Lamented Richard Crowder, a former Duke player: "State had such a stranglehold."

Case had constructed a hardy foundation for his Wolfpack dynasty with talent from his hoops-crazy home state, and several of those Indiana boys made the Dixie Classic their own private playground in the tournament's youth. Two of the most legendary Hoosiers to partner with Case were forwards Dick Dickey and Sam Ranzino, a pair who, the *News and Observer* opined after a 1949 Classic victory over Georgia Tech, "contributed most to the grief of the bewildered Jackets." Each of the two scored in double figures in every game of the inaugural Dixie Classic, and Dickey earned the first MVP trophy and Ranzino took home the second.

Dickey first met Case during World War II, when a Case-led team from an Iowa naval base played against Dickey's team from a California base. A six foot one forward, he was a prolific scorer who popularized the one-handed jumper in the days of underhanded free throws and the two-handed set shot. Ranzino, who came in the year after Dickey, set a new school record for scoring when he poured in 33 points against Rhode Island in the first round of the inaugural Dixie Classic. Known by Case as "The Kid," Ranzino was one of only three three-time All-Americans in Wolfpack history, joining Dickey and David Thompson in that elite company.

The Wolfpack player who left his mark on the third Dixie Classic, in 1951, would figure prominently in the team's future as well. Lee Terrill was the senior team captain that year, and his leadership would come back into play when he served as a Wolfpack assistant coach starting in 1955. Terrill was always a steady presence, a precise passer and a floor leader, but his MVP distinction came from his tenacity in a tight 51–49 win over Cornell in the 1951 final. Terrill only scored six points in the game, but he was credited with directing the defensive freeze that slowed the Big Red's late-game rally.

When Terrill and his teammates cut down the nets that night, they were continuing a hometown tournament dominance that included fifteen straight wins in Southern Conference championships and nine straight in the Dixie Classic that still seemed like the flashy fun toy owned by the luckiest kid on the block.

Not only did State hold the championship for four years, a team from outside North Carolina never took home the Dixie

Classic trophy. But both of those streaks seemed to be in jeopardy on December 30, 1952, when an undefeated Holy Cross team came south bent on relocating the Classic's bragging rights. After dominating North Carolina in the first round, a game in which Holy Cross forward Togo Palazzi tied the tournament rebound record with 31, the Crusaders advanced to the semifinal round against the host team.

"The advance dope has it that the tourney champion will come out of that battle," *News and Observer* columnist Dick Herbert wrote. "Can State beat Holy Cross? That was the question being asked around the Coliseum following yesterday afternoon's program. Coach Everett Case said the Crusaders are 'awfully dangerous.'"

The Wolfpack answered that query with a nail biter that was, up to that point, State's closest contest ever at the Dixie Classic. With six minutes to play, the Wolfpack was trailing by eight points, and the Holy Cross players were already casting themselves as giant killers. But Holy Cross missed some clutch free throws down the stretch, and State center Mel Thompson stepped into the hero role to spark State's push to a 76–74 victory. "It was a bruising, hectic struggle for the full 40 minutes, leaving the crowd of 10,000 exhausted at the finish," Herbert chronicled in the New Year's Eve sports page.

While no one else came so close to unseating the Wolfpack as Holy Cross, a 1950 visiting team shared the court with Duke in the most famous Dixie Classic game ever played by the Blue Devils. The game itself was inconsequential—both teams had suffered defeats in the first round the previous day—but the afternoon's theatrics loom large today because of their historical significance. In coming back from a 32-point deficit to beat Tulane 74–72, Duke still owned the greatest comeback in NCAA history, more than sixty years later.

Leading Duke back from the pit was star guard Dick Groat, who would be named national player of the year the following season. Against Tulane, Groat scored 24 of his 32 points in the second half and 12 in the final four minutes to engineer his team's improbable comeback. The Green Wave did not score a single point in the final eight minutes. The Blue Devils, according to the Raleigh *News and Observer*, "were snatched from the yawning maw of basketball disaster by six-foot Dick Groat."

Groat, who went on to play both professional basketball and major league baseball, vividly remembers how bleak things looked in the Duke locker room at halftime. Coach Hal Bradley attempted a pep talk, but victory wasn't really a goal he was setting before his players at that point. "The second half, everything just seemed to fall into place," Groat said. "Coach Bradley had told us, 'I don't know if you can win this game, but please don't embarrass me.'" Groat's teammate Richard Crowder had fouled out in the third quarter, so he could only yell from the bench as Groat took charge. "We were behind 29 points at the half, about three-fourth of the fans had left to get an early supper, and Dick came alive," Crowder said.

Bill Currie, the longtime radio voice of UNC basketball, was describing the Reynolds Coliseum scene that day for listeners across the Southeast. Decades later, sportswriter Maury Allen would choose Currie's account as one of the most exciting play-by-play calls in college basketball history.

Just a few hours after Duke's amazing comeback, full from that early supper, 12,200 fans watched as N. C. State defeated Colgate for the second Dixie Classic trophy, comprising the largest crowd in tournament history to that point. The following year, the final game would be a sellout of 12,400, and that trend would continue for the remainder of the Dixie Classic's existence. With that trophy, which marked Everett Case's fifth year at the helm of the NCSU team, the Wolfpack kept a remarkable streak alive—the team under Case had never lost any game in a tournament, hauling in four Southern Conference and two Dixie Classic championships.

Even if they left without the trophy, Holy Cross made an impression on Dixie Classic fans by pushing N. C. State to the limit in 1952, but the Crusaders were not the only team that made a memorable visit to Reynolds during those early years. Like Holy Cross, Navy was also undefeated when it fell to the Wolfpack in the first round of the Dixie Classic, and in that same year Cornell gave N. C. State a scare in the finals, cutting State's seven-point lead to one in the final minutes. Mel Thompson was Mr. Clutch that night as well, leading his team with 16 points.

In 1951, Columbia University came to town, still reeling from the point-shaving scandals that had touched all New York City collegiate basketball the year before. The Lions had won twenty-two straight games the previous season but stumbled at the Dixie Classic, losing all three contests despite falling by only two points on the second day and only one point on the third. But Columbia head coach Lou Rossini assured the media that his group would be much tougher come February, when a New York schoolboy named Jack Molinas became eligible. Molinas was serving a six-month suspension for a dorm prank gone wrong, but he was widely regarded as one of the most promising players in the Big Apple. "I wish you could see him," Rossini said. "He is six six, weighs 220 pounds and can outrun any man on the squad."

Molinas might have missed the chance to play in the supercharged Dixie Classic environment, but one of his frequent Ivy League opponents came to Raleigh in 1952 and turned in a performance that is unrivaled in the history of the Classic. His name was Ernie Beck, a Philadelphia native who brought his hoops talents to nearby University of Pennsylvania and stunned the Reynolds Coliseum crowd when he spent Christmas break of his senior year at the Dixie Classic.

Beck's team lost its first game against Wake Forest 65–61, but the six four forward did his part for the Quakers with

25 points. On the second day of competition, Penn lined up against Duke, the championship out of reach for both teams, nothing much at stake. Beck drained 47 points and pulled down 20 rebounds in a performance that still stands as the University of Pennsylvania record for most points in a game and propelled his team to a 97–80 win.

In the final round, Beck took the court against Carolina for the consolation championship, and scored 28 more points for a three-game Dixie Classic record of 100 points. It was a record that shattered Dick Groat's 1950 mark of 79 total points and one that would stand for the duration of the tournament's history. "The matinee crowd paid him a hero's tribute when handsome Howie Dallmar, the Penn coach, removed his star from the action forty-one seconds from the finish. Beck had just tossed in two free throws to reach the century mark," said the next day's *News and Observer* account.

After N.C. State defeated Brigham Young for its fourth tournament crown later that day, Beck was named the most valuable player of the Classic. He would be the only player from a non-North Carolina team to ever earn the MVP distinction. In 2000, he donated his Dixie Classic MVP trophy to the Palestra, the historic Philadelphia arena where the Quakers have played home games since 1927. When the venue underwent a renovation and organizers asked Beck for a piece of Penn history, he could not think of anything better than that reminder of his remarkable trip down South in 1952.

"All I remember is that we were treated very well," said Beck, who credited his Dixie Classic scoring blitz with helping solidify his selection as an All-American later that season. "I remember the food being a little bit different but the treatment was so good. We were northerners. We didn't know anything about the South in those days. We don't like the food down there. But the crowds were full, and Everett Case was really the big man in college basketball."

While his performance has gone down in history, Beck himself always remembered the Wake Forest game that got in the way of his team contending for a Dixie Classic trophy and the great player who had such an arresting presence in the paint, Demon Deacon legend Dickie Hemric. Hemric grew up in tiny Jonesville, North Carolina, and his six foot six inch frame and high school hoops prowess attracted the attention of nearby Wake Forest. He entered WFU in 1951, and had he followed the same path as most college basketball players of that era he would have suited up for a freshman team that year and been forced to wait until he was a sophomore to compete on the varsity. But the Korean War draft was siphoning off so many student-athletes at Wake Forest that the school let Hemric and his classmates play in the big leagues from the beginning, which meant that Hemric was one of the few players to enjoy four Dixie Classics.

He made the most of every one of them, but Hemric left the most indelible impression on his inaugural visit, as a young boy of eighteen with only one semester of college under his belt. His Demon Deacons lost to Duke in the second round behind Dick Groat's 35 points, but Hemric still totaled 31 rebounds for the afternoon, a mark that stands forever as the highest single-game rebounding performance in Dixie Classic history. Hemric also owns the three-day tournament record for most rebounds, with 81, for that same 1951 Classic.

Hemric went on to become the Demon Deacons' all-time scoring leader, with 2,597 career points, and rebound leader with 1,802. That all-time rebounding total also stands as a record in the Atlantic Coast Conference, which formed in 1953 with Wake Forest as a charter member. Hemric bracketed his Dixie Classic experiences by propelling his team to a 96–94 victory over West Virginia in 1954 that was the highest scoring game in Classic history. It was Hemric's senior year, and his farewell gift to the Dixie Classic was 86 total points. In the West Virginia game, which saw Mountaineers star Rod Hundley tie Beck's single-game record with 47 points, Hemric scored 35 and grabbed 20 rebounds.

But for all of his record-felling theatrics, the Dixie Classic win that might have given Hemric the most satisfaction came in the consolation final of the 1953 tournament. On the previous afternoon, Navy had ended N. C. State's run of Dixie Classic domination by defeating the Wolfpack 85–75 in the second round. On the final day, in the battle for third place, Hemric-led Wake Forest finished what the Middies started and beat State 86–79. Hemric scored 24 points as the Demon Deacons became the first team in the Big Four to topple the tournament hosts.

"Of all the holiday tournaments, I think I fed off of that one the most," said Hemric. "We would move to a motel between Wake Forest and Raleigh and stay there for the three-day tournament. I remember like yesterday all of those people coming in, and they would be out in the parking lot—tailgating in the Reynolds Coliseum parking lot."

Wake Forest's 1953 win over State, while historic in the Dixie Classic environs, was actually just one of many chinks in the armor which had protected N. C. State from defeat in tournament play through Everett Case's first six years as head coach. In the previous regular season, both Wake Forest and North Carolina had defeated N. C. State in games decided by only a single point. The Demon Deacons' win on December 9, 1952, was their first over the Wolfpack since 1948, and the Tar Heels' victory on January 24, 1953, was the first since the Case era had begun in 1946. But Wake Forest, with Hemric holding up the center, was proving to have N. C. State's number. The Demon Deacons defeated the Wolfpack again on March 7, 1953, again by only one point, in the finals of the Southern Conference Tournament. It was Wake's first victory over State in Reynolds, and the Dixie Classic win that same December would be the second.

The two teams' rivalry dated back to 1911, when N. C. State played its first-ever collegiate basketball game against Wake Forest—a mere twenty years after Dr. James Naismith invented the game in Massachusetts. It was a relationship that inspired more passion in those years than any other among the Big Four, and Wake Forest's rise was the first signal that Everett Case's quest to bring basketball fervor to North Carolina was working. He was, in a sense, tripping over his own successful mission, as the other teams on Tobacco Road started elevating their game and extending their recruiting reach to basketball hot spots like Indiana and New York in their efforts to prune N. C. State's budding dynasty.

"We owe a lot to Everett Case, we the basketball world, for creating the demand for big-time basketball," Hemric said. "I want to think that Wake Forest was the start of his decline."

Jack Murdock, who starred for WFU in the mid-fifties, grew up in Raleigh as an avid Dixie Classic fan, but the only two schools that offered him basketball scholarships in 1953 were Duke and Wake Forest. As he put it, he chose the Baptists over the Methodists, and competed for the Demon Deacons during the years when parity, rather than Wolfpack supremacy, was the order of things among the Big Four. Of Case, Murdock said, "He made others change. He came in, and nobody could beat him, so they started competing harder."

The progressive rise of the other three-fourths of the Big Four only served to spotlight North Carolina's new position as one of the nation's hoops epicenters. And since fans from all four schools lived in and near Raleigh, the hubbub surrounding the Dixie Classic only increased when contests between Tobacco Road schools went from foregone conclusions to edge-of-the-seat battles. In the first six years of the Classic, every final game included one Big Four team and one out-of-state team, and in five of those years the local team was N. C. State. But in the second six years of the tournament, only one outside team—Michigan State in 1958—contested the title. Every other year the final game, which was often held on New Year's Eve, unfolded as a drama between two neighbors.

For three straight years of the tournament—1955, 1956, and 1957—the Big Four suspended their southern hospitality to completely shut their visitors out of trophy contention. For each of those years, the North Carolina teams played in both the championship final and the consolation final. Dave Odom was a boy living in nearby Goldsboro during those years, and he never missed a Dixie Classic. His father's good friend Raymond Bryan was a big Wolfpack booster who always gave Odom and his father two full books of Classic tickets, and he remembers vividly where they sat—section 12, row B, in the balcony right next to the box reserved for the North Carolina governor. One of the brightest highlights out of many for Odom and other fans was the chance to sit through the evening doubleheader on the second day or—even better—the final day, and watch only the Wolfpack, Blue Devils, Tar Heels, and Demon Deacons.

Odom, who later became the head coach of Wake Forest and South Carolina, said, "The greatest day of all was at the end of that first day, if all four of the Big Four teams were able to win, and go into that second day, in the semifinals at night, and play against each other at night. And then you could really draw the lines of allegiance, and then you began to fight for superiority."

The majority of the tournament hardware was assured of staying in the Tar Heel State. Beck was the only MVP from elsewhere, and the first three—Dick Dickey, Sam Ranzino, and Lee Terrill—were all on Case's N. C. State squads. Six teams, Penn State in 1949, Colgate in 1950, Cornell in 1951, Brigham Young in 1952, Navy in 1953, and Minnesota in 1954, won second place in the early years before the Big Four shut them out, and only three teams from outside the state ever won the third-place consolation trophy—Rhode Island State in 1949, Dayton in 1959, and Villanova in 1960.

As Case's teams lost their iron grip on the Dixie Classic, the fans like Odom were the winners. The rise of neighboring programs—and Case's continuing efforts to bring in the top teams from out of state—led to an event that was rocketing in popularity. It had become, far and away, the most popular collegiate holiday basketball tournament ever staged.

The holiday break had long been the domain of high school tournaments, but the Classic's success gave rise to other collegiate events as well. The most famous of these was the Holiday Festival in Madison Square Garden, which started in 1952 with Utah State beating Manhattan for the first-ever championship. The Festival, which started with an eight-team field like the Dixie Classic, is still played today with a four-team field. The majority of the Holiday Festival participants in the 1950s and 1960s hailed from schools in the Northeast, and a team from North Carolina did not accept an invitation until 1968, when the UNC Tar Heels made the trip.

More famously, Madison Square Garden was host to the National Invitational Tournament (NIT), which was started in 1938 to crown college basketball's top team. The NCAA started its own championship the following year in Evanston, Illinois, and for decades the tournaments invited teams independently of one another, meaning that it was possible for the same team to win both titles. In those early years, though, the NIT carried more prestige because of its setting, the historic Garden, which from college basketball's infancy had pitted top teams against one another and became the special showcase of emerging Big Apple teams like St. John's, City College of New York, and Long Island University.

An invitation to play in the Garden was always special for a team from the South, and Case's N. C. State teams had some memorable trips there, like the 1950 NCAA regional that brought them victories over Holy Cross and Baylor and a loss to City College of New York, the team that would go on to become the only team in history to win both the NCAA and NIT tournaments. But even as the Dixie Classic was becoming the Old North State's most diverting holiday tradition, Case was inspiring a trend that would take the personalities and basketball savvy of the Big Apple and give them a home right there on Tobacco Road.

Four

Everett Case was a midwesterner born and bred, but it was soon clear that he belonged to the state of North Carolina. His grandiose visions of how big basketball could be, his innovative approach to preparation and play, and his single-minded devotion to his sport and his Wolfpack team all combined to make him a pied piper of the hardwood, not just for N. C. State but for the other Big Four schools as well.

Some twenty miles west of Raleigh, in the quaint burg of Chapel Hill, University of North Carolina athletic officials were trying to figure out how to harness some Case magic of their own. The basketball team at the oldest state university in the nation was foundering. Head coach Tom Scott had taken the helm of the team then known as the White Phantoms in 1946, the same year that Case put down roots in Raleigh. But the similarities between the two coaching chapters ended there. Scott inherited a team that was fresh off of a loss in the 1946 NCAA Tournament final, but even though his squads put together winning records for four of his six seasons, they never advanced past the Southern Conference Tournament. And the mountain standing in their way was, of course, Everett Case and his Wolfpack.

In sports parlance, N. C. State quite simply had Carolina's number. The Tar Heels never prevailed against the Wolfpack under Coach Scott; they lost a debilitating fifteen straight games, including four in tournaments like the Dixie Classic and the Southern Conference championship that determined a berth in the NCAA Tournament. After Carolina went 12–15 for the second straight year in 1951–52, UNC officials and Scott mutually agreed that he should seek other opportunities. The coaching search that ensued set a new course in Tar Heel basketball history and gave Chapel Hill its own larger-than-life coach—a slick New Yorker named Frank McGuire.

McGuire had spent five years coaching both basketball and baseball at his alma mater, St. John's University, and in 1952 his Redmen advanced to the NCAA Final Four. Lennie Rosenbluth, a New York high school phenom at the time who knew McGuire through his father, remembered attending a testimonial dinner lauding McGuire's accomplishments and hearing rumors that McGuire was considering a move south. He was deciding, it was reported, between Alabama and North Carolina.

A friend of former UNC coach Ben Carnevale, McGuire had spent time on the Chapel Hill campus in pre-flight training for the navy during World War II, and it seemed to him like an ideal place to build a new dynasty and escape the congestion of the Big Apple. From the moment he arrived, he established a reputation as an astute basketball mind and a sharp dresser, and Carolina fans looked to him as the general who could lead them into victory against the redcoats down the road.

"McGuire was all New York City, unlike anything North Carolina had previously seen," Ron Morris wrote in *ACC Basketball: An Illustrated History*. "His suit was perfectly tailored, his white shirt starched and crisp against his chest with his necktie pulled tight. As he adjusted the red scarf in his jacket pocket and flashed his diamond cuff links, every head turned to notice the coach lauded by one magazine as 'one of America's best-dressed men.'" Dave Odom was just a boy when McGuire arrived, and a State fan to boot, but six decades later he could vividly remember the image of the coach fastidiously adjusting his cuff links before a game.

Fresh off his greatest St. John's success, McGuire's departure from the city was a surprise to many observers, and those close to him cited his son Frankie's medical situation—he had cerebral palsy—as a chief reason for the move. But McGuire was really just one piece of a mass exodus that started in 1951, the bleakest year in New York basketball history, and marked the decline of the city that had epitomized college hoops glory.

In the thirties and forties, New York was a basketball Mecca, as Madison Square Garden became the ultimate competitive venue and the colleges in the five boroughs competed for the outstanding players forged on the blacktops of the city's playgrounds. Long Island University and St. John's both won the NIT championship in the forties, and with the exception of Kentucky and Indiana most of the high-level basketball in the country was being played in New York. Long Island University, New York University, Columbia, and St. John's all enjoyed moments of triumph, but no accomplishment better represented the pinnacle of the New York basketball era than City College of New York's 1950 sweep of both the NIT and the NCAA championships. City College, a tuition-free school that chose students for academic, not athletic excellence, was the only team in history to win both major tournaments.

But CCNY fell from grace swiftly the year after its sweep, when in the first four months of 1951 nineteen players from four colleges were arrested for conspiring to fix basketball games in which they had competed. Four of the players who confessed to plotting with gamblers to manipulate the outcome of games were part of the starting five of the CCNY championship squad. "The romance was over," wrote Stanley Cohen in his book about the New York scandals, *The Game They Played*. "The love affair between New York City and basketball had been tarnished by deception, and the city reacted with the indifferent hostility of a betrayed lover."

The most prominent player whose name was muddied in the scandal was Long Island University's Sherman White, named national player of the year by *The Sporting News* just months before he confessed to working with two teammates to manipulate the outcome of four games. (One of the fixed games, on January 17, 1950, was a 55–52 LIU loss to N. C. State in Madison Square Garden.)

Whispers of gambling had swirled around college basketball since at least 1931, when a St. John's player named Max Posnack was reportedly offered $3,000 to throw a game against Manhattan College. But the development that really piqued the interest of bookmakers and their clients was the introduction of the "line," or the "spread," in the early 1940s. Basketball games went from a straight-odds wager to a vista of betting possibilities, because the point spread evened out the differences between the teams. For instance, if NYU was a seven-and-a-half point favorite over St. John's, then the favorite had to win by eight or more for its backers to collect, and a victory of seven or less meant a windfall for those who had bet on the underdog.

The point spread also created ethical gray areas for players drawn by the notion of making a quick fortune. It's easy to pull off and virtually impossible to detect, the gamblers would tell them. You don't have to lose the game—you only have to make sure that your team stays within the spread.

"Basketball soon became the most heavily bet sport in America," Cohen wrote. "The spread was the gambler's delight and every balm to the bookmaker. It made every game a toss-up. It also made it possible for a team to win a game on the board and still lose it to the points. What difference did it make whether the team won by seven or five? The player would be able to win twice—he could win both the game and the bet—not by dumping, but by shaving the points. One could make his pact with the devil and still remain on the side of the angels. Wasn't that the Great American Dream?"

As one point-shaving allegation after another was made in early 1951, sixty-eight New York detectives were assigned to bring down the gamblers and players who had marred the game. They recovered more than $26,000 in bribe money, and when their investigation was closed it would reveal that at least two dozen games from 1949 to 1951 had been fixed. Just a month after the CCNY players and their counterparts from LIU, NYU, and Manhattan College had confessed, the NIT invitations were attracting little interest, and the ever-popular Madison Square Garden doubleheaders drew paltry crowds. When that season of scandal drew to a close and top players and coaches in the Big Apple evaluated their future in the sport, the greener pastures suddenly seemed to lie outside the borders of the Empire State.

Rosenbluth, who looked up to McGuire and had long dreamed of being a New York superstar with a following in the Garden, was one of many young players who started to expand their horizons. "None of the players wanted to stay in New York, because basketball wasn't there anymore," Rosenbluth said.

As every city basketball triumph took on a shadow and New York heroes became goats overnight, Frank McGuire's St. John's program remained above the fray. Of the five schools that played part of their home schedule in Madison Square Garden, the Redmen were the only team that emerged from that dark time with no allegations of conspiring with gamblers. There were murmurs that the program was involved but protected by New York's powerful Catholic Church officials, but those suspicions were never proven. McGuire led his team to the Final Four in 1952, the year after the scandals, and then beat a path south to Chapel Hill.

He may not have conspired with gamblers or the Mafia members who often underwrote their activities, but no one who knew him disputes that McGuire probably associated with some of the characters who engineered those deals. The son of a city cop, he always kept close associations with both the law and the Mob. Joel Fleishman, who was the UNC manager in the mid-fifties, remembers when McGuire asked him to call Madison Square Garden to request more tickets for an NCAA playoff game between the Tar Heels and the Yale Bulldogs. The Garden officials tried to tell Fleishman that it would be better to secure one block of seats for McGuire's family and friends, but he pushed for two separate sections on opposite ends of the arena. "I said, 'No, no, you don't get it,'" Fleishman remembered. "We have the cops and the priests on one side and the Mob and the convicts on the other side."

McGuire's arrival heralded a new day around the UNC campus, and the Tar Heels prevailed in their first four games under their new coach. Then McGuire took his undefeated team to his first Dixie Classic in 1952 and drew the powerful Holy Cross team that almost unseated the Wolfpack in the second round. The Crusaders handed McGuire his first loss, and UNC went 1–2 in the tournament, defeating Princeton in the second round and losing to Penn and its high-scoring star Ernie Beck in the consolation finals.

But the Tar Heels did not stay down for long. After winning six straight in January, they traveled back to Reynolds Coliseum in February of 1953 and stunned their rivals, 70–69. It was UNC's first victory over N. C. State in nearly six years, and while the tide had not fully turned—the Wolfpack would win the next six games in the series—it unburdened Carolina fans of the idea that they would always play second fiddle to N. C. State. It was one of McGuire's few triumphant moments in an arena that, to him, came to represent an unjust chasm between his program and Case's.

The Tar Heels played in Woollen Gym, an unspectacular structure built in 1938 with half the capacity of Reynolds Coliseum. McGuire's first game as head coach attracted only 1,200 fans, and his early teams sometimes slept on cots in their opponents' gyms for away games and traveled to those distant cities crowded into private cars.

Of course, a disproportionate number of the road trips were only twenty miles away, in the capital city of Raleigh. Thanks to Case's insistence that his arena be the biggest in the Southeast and his enthusiasm for tournaments like the Dixie Classic and the Southern Conference championship, teams like UNC found themselves playing as many games in Reynolds as they did on their home floor. Former Tar Heel player Pete Brennan remembers one season when his team played seven games in Raleigh and only eight in Woollen Gym. McGuire, whose first office on the Carolina campus was a converted ticket booth that he shared with his assistant, grumbled often about his subpar facilities and the edge enjoyed by a team with a giant organ, a noise meter, and 12,400 seats. The sum of those inequities also served to fuel one of the most intriguing relationships during that era—the personal rivalry between McGuire and Case.

The much-touted friction between the two coaches may have contained a kernel of true animosity, but most of the people on the inside of the two programs contended that it was more of a publicity stunt than anything. When Lennie Rosenbluth was playing at UNC for McGuire, he remembers rumors that his coach liked to join Everett Case for breakfast on Sundays, and some speculated that they dreamed up new ways to fuel their rivalry. Case, the master promoter, and McGuire, the spirited New Yorker, knew that cordial vanilla friendships between coaches did not inspire passion or sell tickets. "Coach McGuire was a good old Irishman from Hell's Kitchen, and there's nothing he enjoyed more than a little controversy," Joel Fleishman said.

If it was an act, it was well-played. After one 1954 NCSU win over Carolina, the coaches declined to shake hands. After another decisive Wolfpack victory, McGuire complained that

Case had ruined the game of basketball by employing a full-court press, which prompted Case to respond: "Since when did he get to the place where he could coach my ball club? I'll do anything I please as long as it's within the rules."

McGuire, who as a St. John's player once threatened to fight the entire Providence College team, railed against that full-court press by declaring, "I'll never forget this night. The tide will turn some day. You can quote me as saying I am declaring open war against Everett Case ... I thought he was my friend, but I know better now. I just can't wait until the day comes when I can meet him on equal terms. I'll get even with that rascal."

The atmosphere between Raleigh and Chapel Hill kept getting hotter, and as the Tar Heels' confidence grew so did their conviction that they could be crashers to the Wolfpack's annual holiday party at Reynolds Coliseum. Wake Forest had the distinction of being the first Big Four team to topple the hosts at the Dixie Classic, prevailing 86–79 in the consolation round in 1953. McGuire's team was slower to gain a foothold in the event, falling to the Wolfpack in 1954 and 1955. The two teams did not meet again until 1957, but it was the championship game, and McGuire finally asserted himself on Case's favorite stage, leading his team to victory in a 39–30 defensive battle. By the time they finally defeated the Wolfpack in the Classic, though, the Tar Heels had already beaten Case to the biggest prize of all, a national championship. The parity among the Big Four squads was creating a compelling annual dance that fueled fan passion and electrified every tournament where all four teams were competing.

McGuire never lost his big-city flair or his Bronx brashness, but as he became more at home in the Tar Heel State he attracted more and more fellow New Yorkers to try their hand on the emerging southern hoops scene. New York was where McGuire knew people, so New York was where he turned to recruit most of his biggest stars in those early years. And his very first recruiting project was a lanky Jewish boy named Lennie Rosenbluth.

Because of his father's friendship with McGuire, Rosenbluth had watched the coach operate since he was a boy, frequenting Madison Square Garden during McGuire's St. John's years. But ironically, the first North Carolina coach to woo Rosenbluth was none other than Everett Case. The versatile six foot five Rosenbluth was bent on getting out of New York in the wake of the city basketball scandals, and N. C. State was at the top of his wish list. He visited the campus in Raleigh as a high school junior, but he did not play well in an impromptu tryout arranged by Case, and no scholarship offer came.

Rosenbluth's redemption came from McGuire, who let him know as soon as he signed his coaching contract with North Carolina that he wanted Rosenbluth to become a Tar Heel. Rosenbluth had to go to prep school for a year to fulfill the academic requirements he needed to enter college, and in 1953, a year after his old friend, he arrived in Chapel Hill. He was followed by other New Yorker-turned-Tar Heel legends via what became known as McGuire's "Underground Railroad"—Bob Young, Joe Quigg, Pete Brennan, Bob Cunningham, Tommy Kearns, and others whose talent helped spark a UNC basketball renaissance. McGuire never apologized for mining his home city's playgrounds and high school gyms, even if some of those guys got on a train without any idea where they were actually going to spend four years.

"Someone asked me, 'Where are you going?'" Rosenbluth recalled. "I said, 'University of North Carolina.' I didn't know where that was. I didn't have a clue, until I came down here."

In a *Sports Illustrated* article about his recruiting tactics, McGuire served notice to other coaches who hoped to capitalize on New York's basketball depth: "New York is my personal territory," McGuire said. "Duke can scout in Philadelphia and

North Carolina State can have the whole country. But if anybody wants to move into New York, they need a passport from me. All the people in New York are my friends. No one gets paid for helping, but everybody looks out for me. The whole police department looks for players for me. So do the high school coaches, so do the brothers at the Catholic schools."

McGuire had his ways of making prospective players' parents feel at ease about sending their teenage sons a thousand miles from home. Pete Brennan grew up in a devout Catholic family, and his father's lifelong dream had his son attending Notre Dame. But then McGuire swept through in his Italian suit with a slick marketing presentation about the opportunities for Brennan down South. The kicker: He promised Brennan's father that he would make sure Pete attended Mass. "On the third visit he told my parents, 'If Pete will come to Chapel Hill, I'll make sure he goes to church every Sunday,'" Brennan said. "And I went every Sunday—but I never saw McGuire there."

Their coach might have bristled at the Tar Heels' frequent trips to Raleigh, but the New York players enjoyed Reynolds Coliseum and its atmosphere, which was reminiscent of Madison Square Garden in its glory days. Tar Heel player Bob Young liked the crowds, which were infused with more and more light blue as McGuire's winning habits inspired fan support. And the floor was superior to most of the others the teams competed on, especially their home court at Woollen Gym, Brennan said. "I loved the court over there [at Reynolds] because in Chapel Hill, they had the concrete right under the wood. But in Reynolds Coliseum they had the removable floor, one of the few we played on, and it really had spring in it. So I loved playing there."

The Dixie Classic, in particular, evoked fond memories for the riders on McGuire's Underground Railroad. Rosenbluth's Tar Heels did not bring home the ultimate prize from the tournament until his senior year, but he always looked forward to the spectacle, even if it prevented him and his Yankee team-mates from spending the holiday season at home. "It was a fantastic three days of basketball," he said. "It was great. It was a great tournament for the fans. The ballplayers loved it too, but the Dixie Classic was for the people of North Carolina."

The Classic became the toughest tournament ticket to get by the mid-fifties, but it wasn't the only important tournament for the Big Four and its loyal fans. Before 1953, the Southern Conference held its championship event every March with high stakes—only the winner would earn a berth in the NCAA Tournament. But after the 1952–53 season concluded, Big Four athletic officials made a decision that would up the ante between the Tobacco Road rivals and lead to the creation of a tournament that would become the most enduringly popular event in North Carolina basketball history.

The birth of the Atlantic Coast Conference in 1953 had more to do with football than anything else, but basketball fans were the truest beneficiaries of the new organization, which consisted of seven members of the Southern Conference—N. C. State, UNC, Duke, Wake Forest, Maryland, Clemson, and South Carolina. Later that year the University of Virginia was admitted to the league. Like it had for the Southern Conference, N. C. State offered to host the league tournament, and the first thirteen ACC Tournaments were played at Reynolds Coliseum. The home team mimicked its Dixie Classic trend by winning the first three trophies before North Carolina broke the streak in 1957.

With Frank McGuire ensconced in his tiny office down the road, Everett Case was slowly becoming a victim of his own success. Big Four fans, whose passion for basketball seemed boundless, loved the Dixie Classic and were starting to see the appeal of the ACC Tournament. But they wanted more excitement, more last-second shots, and more overtime games. They wanted Demon Deacons, Blue Devils, and Tar Heels to find their own places on the national stage. They didn't mind flocking to the house that Case built to enjoy the grand events he created in that arena. But more and more, they longed to topple the Wolfpack and start their own trophy collection to rival Case's. In 1953, a year after Frank McGuire came south and just months after the ACC was formed, the Dixie Classic hardware finally left Raleigh, bound for an unexpected destination.

Five

It wasn't just Frank McGuire's southern migration that signaled the shift from Wolfpack supremacy to rivalries among equals. The most significant coup in the battle to topple N. C. State came quietly, from an unassuming coach at the Methodist school best known for its football team.

The fifth Dixie Classic, which opened on December 28, 1953, had all of the earmarks of another State sweep. Raleigh sportswriter Dick Herbert pronounced it the strongest Dixie Classic field in history, with North Carolina and Navy both coming in undefeated and Oregon State ranked fourth in the nation and coming off a decisive win over defending national champion Indiana. The Wolfpack had compiled an 8–1 record and seemed to be recovering from a road loss to Wake Forest in early December. They were favored in their first-round match-up against Seton Hall.

About the Blue Devils, who were paired against Oregon State in the first round, Herbert wrote, "Duke never has performed well in the Classic, but Coach Hal Bradley again has a high scoring outfit that got off to a better start this season. Whether it can handle the Beavers' height, though, is a big question." Oregon State's star center, Wade Halbrook, was seven foot three inches, almost unheard of in an era when starting forwards were typically shorter than six four.

Even without Halbrook, the Beavers would have been the tallest team in the Dixie Classic field, but Duke surprised the prognosticators with a stellar shooting performance and an inventive defense that held Halbrook, called "the tallest basketball player in captivity," to 23 points. Bradley's game plan included a fast offensive attack that capitalized on the skills of guards Joe Belmont and Rudy D'Emilio, who each put in 19 points for the Blue Devils. Duke had never won in the first round of the Dixie Classic before, and this milestone was a decided upset. "The Beavers perhaps felt the effects of their long road trip, for they were guilty of numerous traveling violations and fumbles," Herbert wrote on December 29. "Duke, meanwhile, played at a steady pace throughout and offered a balanced attack."

Also in the first round, N. C. State slipped past Seton Hall 72–70 in a game which saw the Wolfpack trailing by eight points late in the contest. State's second round matchup would pair them with Navy, the team that dispatched North Carolina 86–62 in the first round behind Midshipmen center Don Lange's 29 points. The favorite now that Oregon State was eliminated from the championship bracket, N. C. State would line up against Navy in the second round.

And it was the boys in uniform from Annapolis that finally did what no Big Four team had yet to do: knock off the hosts of the Dixie Classic. The Middies, propped up by the shooting of Lange and John Clune, prevailed 85–75 despite a seven-point Wolfpack lead at halftime. The victory was credited to the second-half strategy of Navy coach Ben Carnevale, the former North Carolina head coach who helped lure Frank McGuire south. "State's dominance of the Dixie Classic has ended," declared writer Mac McDuffie in the *News and Observer*. In the evening session after State's misstep, the Blue Devils, emboldened by their first-round triumph, defeated Wake Forest 83–66 to set up an unlikely final between Duke and Navy.

"Unbeaten Navy and unpredictable Duke shocked 20,000 Dixie Classic spectators here this afternoon and tonight to advance, totally unexpected, into the finals of this holiday basketball tournament," Greensboro *News and Record* sportswriter Irwin Smallwood wrote.

What followed on December 30 was certainly one of the most unforgettable career highlights for Hal Bradley, Duke's placid coach who came to Durham in 1950 to replace Gerry Gerard when Gerard became ill with cancer. Bradley's eight-year stint was stable, if unremarkable, but when his team defeated Navy 98–83 to become the first team from outside of Raleigh to claim the Dixie Classic trophy, he celebrated with gusto. "Beside themselves with joy, the Duke players rushed to their bench and swept Bradley to their shoulders," recorded the *News and Observer*. "They carried him to the Coliseum's south goal and from somewhere somebody produced a pair of scissors. Bradley clipped the hoop as clean as a baby's cheek in the traditional net-cutting privilege which goes to the conquerors."

The star for Duke, and the tournament MVP, was senior guard Rudy D'Emilio, who contributed 24 points. But Duke's victory, which set a Reynolds Coliseum and Dixie Classic record for most points scored, was truly a team effort, with four players turning in double digits and D'Emilio's fellow guard sophomore Joe Belmont scoring 22. Propelled by that early-season triumph, Duke went on to a 22–6 record that season and finished first in the regular-season standings for the brand-new Atlantic Coast Conference. But they stumbled in the semifinals of the ACC tournament to N. C. State, cancelling any hopes to make their mark on the postseason.

When the Dixie Classic Queen had handed out her last trophy at the 1953 event, the coach of the team who had traveled the farthest to compete and carried some of the highest expectations stood humbled by the tournament that was becoming known as a true test of a basketball team's chops. Slats Gill and his Oregon State Beavers came in with their Number Four ranking and their seven foot three center favored to win, and it was only an abysmal offensive start from North Carolina in the final round—the Tar Heels sunk only 17 points in the first half—that handed the Beavers seventh place rather than last. Before his team boarded their plane for points northwest, Gill lauded the talent on display in the Dixie Classic field.

"My boys learned more here than they could have in a month of scheduled play," Gill said. "It was the greatest tournament I've ever had a team in, and you can call the team that wins one of the best in the nation."

Obscured by Duke's feat in 1953 was another accomplishment by a Big Four team, one that had more to do with bragging rights than trophies. After Navy felled the mighty Wolfpack in the second round, Wake Forest swept in on the final day and handed the hosts another loss, winning third place in the event and becoming the first team from within the state to defeat N. C. State at its signature tournament. Dickie Hemric had 24 points and Al DePorter and Billy Lyles poured in 20 each in the 86–79 win, giving the Demon Deacons their fourth victory over their Raleigh rivals in five tries and officially serving notice of the Wolfpack dynasty's collapse.

Every rivalry within the Big Four has had peaks and valleys, and in the 1950s the war between N. C. State and Wake Forest was at its zenith. Because the Demon Deacons were the first to make sustained trouble for Everett Case, games between the two teams were injected with extra intensity. And it was no coincidence that Wake Forest's profile started to rise right around the time they hired a flamboyant assistant coach whose name would someday be synonymous with Wake Forest basketball—Horace Albert "Bones" McKinney.

Bones became a Demon Deacon icon despite strong early associations with every other Big Four school. He grew up in Durham, literally across the street from Duke, and he always dreamed of going there to play basketball. But Bob Warren, then the coach at N. C. State, recruited the six foot six inch McKinney more aggressively so he signed on with the

Wolfpack. After two years at N. C. State, McKinney was drafted into the military, and he spent eighteen months serving and playing basketball close to home at Fort Bragg in Fayetteville, North Carolina. After the war, Warren had left N. C. State and McKinney had befriended UNC coach Ben Carnevale, so he moved down the road to Chapel Hill and finished his collegiate career as a Tar Heel. He entered the fledgling NBA, playing for the Boston Celtics and the Washington Capitals for six seasons, but by 1952 it was clear that his professional career was ending and he was being called to a drastic career redirection—one that would start by attending a Southern Baptist seminary.

Bones wanted to be a minister, so with his wife Edna and their four children he moved to Wake Forest, North Carolina, to enroll in the very first class at the seminary that shared a campus with Wake Forest University. WFU's head basketball coach, Murray Greason, heard quickly that McKinney was in town, and on the first day of seminary classes he went and waited outside the building for Bones to come out. "My father said, 'Bones, how are you going to support those four children while you go to seminary?'" recalled Murray Greason, Jr., who grew up on the old Wake Forest campus less than one hundred yards from Gore Gymnasium. "And Bones said, 'I got me a paper route.' My father said, 'How would you like to be an assistant coach?'"

The pair went straight to the office of athletic director Jim Weaver, and even though the salary offered to Bones—$750 for the remainder of the season—was considerably less than he had anticipated, McKinney signed on to work with Greason. He immediately took a young player named Dickie Hemric under his wing and taught him some footwork and techniques that were novel to big men in those days, who typically planted themselves predictably under the basket. "Bones taught Hemric the drop step and made my father coach of the year," Greason, Jr., said.

Bones would be Greason's assistant coach for six seasons before taking the head coaching position in 1958, but even as an assistant he was larger than life. Everybody had a Bones McKinney story, whether it was the *Life* magazine photographer who witnessed him making fifty trips to the water cooler during a 1953 Dixie Classic game, or the time he stopped dribbling the ball in a Celtics exhibition game to grab a handful of a fan's popcorn.

"I plead guilty to driving through life at about eighty miles an hour, drinking sixty thousand Pepsi-Colas, smoking some two million cigarettes and threatening the lives of several hundred referees," McKinney wrote in his 1988 autobiography. He completed his seminary education and became an ordained Baptist minister, even conducting the weddings of dozens of Wake Forest players, but he was as well-known for his salty language and hyperkinetic bench antics as he was for his Bible knowledge. "I could never sit still on a bench," McKinney wrote. "I was like a combination yo-yo and elevator—up and down, up and down. I was like a box of corn all popping at the same time. I had to either be running for the water bucket, diagramming some play on the floor, tossing a towel in the air or chasing down a referee."

Bones was an instant attraction at tournaments like the Dixie Classic, where the coaches of the Big Four seemed to hold court at the center of the spectacle. Charlie Bryant, who was a Wake Forest assistant coach under McKinney, said that Bones was a media darling before the age when television would have made him a national celebrity. "Bones was just nuts," Bryant said. "He was absolutely nuts. He was a laugh a minute. If he were living today, he would make so much money he couldn't count it all."

As colorful as he was, Bones's reputation in college basketball was based on far more than his quirks. He had an innovative basketball mind and a natural gift for coaching, and it wasn't long before his methods were being discussed among rival coaches. The Demon Deacons began to notch victories using a Bones-inspired 1-3-1 zone defense, and N. C. State assistant coach Vic Bubas called him one day and asked him if he could come learn the zone and some of the big-man techniques that made Dickie Hemric the two-time ACC Player of the Year. Bones agreed, even if years later he joked with Case and Bubas that he never would have shared his knowledge with them if he had known that the Wolfpack would use it to beat him. "Bones said that Bubas asked him to show him the principles of that defense," said Maurice George, who played for Wake Forest from 1951 to 1954. "Bones said, 'Yeah, I didn't invent it.' But he did. Bones called it 'fruit basket.' It worked perfectly because of our personnel."

The Demon Deacons were the first Big Four team to effectively stop an opponent using a zone defense, and in the early fifties, when McKinney was finding his place as an assistant and Wake began to have N. C. State's number more often than not, the zone gave Case pause. The younger Greason remembered Case telling a reporter that Greason's father, the WFU head coach, was going to ruin basketball with zone defenses. Along with the sharp shooting of Hemric, the zone was certainly one of the forces behind Wake's 1953 Dixie Classic victory over the Wolfpack.

As Wake Forest and Duke collaborated to make the Dixie Classic a newly equalized playing field, fan fervor around the tournament intensified. Tickets were coveted and scarce, and no group set its sights more zealously on obtaining Classic passes than hoops-crazed boys counting down the days to Christmas. For boys in certain pockets of North Carolina, the most prized holiday acquisition was a small stocking stuffer made of paper. Some young fans, like George Whitfield, held that gift in their memory above any bicycle or BB gun that ever came their way. "It was a prize to get a hold of a ticket," remembered Whitfield, who kept his ticket book, which sold for $12.50 for all games, in his bookshelf for six decades after that tournament. "I loved it better than anything in the world."

Smedes York's father was a prominent Raleigh developer and the city's mayor for a while, and York knew that Dixie Classic tickets were a holiday priority for his dad. But even if they had access to the tickets, his father was wise enough to engage in a little behavioral modification, using the coveted tickets as bait. "They would be in my stocking for Christmas. If we did anything wrong, he would threaten to not have the tickets in the stockings."

The parents who arranged for such a surprise were shrewd shoppers indeed, for tickets to the Classic were nearly impossible to come by. Bill Hensley handled media relations for the tournament for five years, and his personal popularity surged every autumn as the big event drew near. But even though some 75,000 people a year gained entry to Reynolds Coliseum during those three days, Hensley wasn't given access to any of the sought-after tickets.

"For about a month before the tournament each year I would get not dozens of calls, but hundreds of calls," Hensley said. "If you'd ever met me before in your life, I would get calls saying, 'I was in Sunday school with you when we were six, and you might not remember me, but I would sure love some Dixie Classic tickets.' I was offered money, gifts—a friend who owned a sporting goods store sent me a shotgun. It was the biggest sporting event I've ever been a part of."

"People were just clamoring," laughed Harry Stewart, who as the head of the Wolfpack Club had access to prime seats. "I had one man bring me a goose one time. It was dead, of course. I said, 'I appreciate it, but I really can't accept anything like this. But I'm also director of the dining hall, so we'll use it at the dining hall."

For basketball fans who were coming of age in the 1950s, the tales of Dixie Classic adventures became like heirlooms, passed down for decades. Dorsey Tyndall was a thirteen-year-old basketball fanatic from Kinston, North Carolina, who had the good fortune to know former UNC player Bob Cunningham and local businessman Charlie McCaskill, a leader in UNC's Rams Club. The two obtained a bunch of tickets to the 1958 Dixie Classic and invited Tyndall and his young friends for the sports trip of a lifetime. "That was something," Tyndall said, "We were very fortunate to be able to do that."

Statistical evidence of the Classic's mushrooming popularity came each year after the tournament, when attendance figures were released. Crowd numbers went up every year with one exception—a slight dip from 1958 to 1959. But in the early years, the line graph was a gently sloping hill, with virtually all of the sessions boasting a full house of 12,400 except, typically, the final afternoon session, where the bottom two teams played each other to avoid the "booby prize." The all-time attendance record was set in 1960, the final year of the tournament, with 73,800 total people attending. Five of the six sessions brought in capacity crowds of 12,400, and the Wednesday afternoon session that year drew 11,800.

The fans might have been shrouded in cigarette smoke, but they were typically a well-heeled bunch, with men coming in suits and ties and women wearing fine dresses and hats. Local businessmen often used the Classic as an opportunity to entertain their most important clients.

Woody Durham was just a boy, years from becoming a regional celebrity as the play-by-play voice of Tar Heel basketball, and so he was never sure he would get into Reynolds for the Dixie Classic. His father had tickets, but he had to offer some of them to business associates. Durham would wait breathlessly, hoping that no deals had to be closed at the Dixie Classic that day, no clients had to be entertained, so that one of the priceless tickets might land in his hands. "It was a great event," Durham said. "It was an extravaganza. People would set their calendars to come to Raleigh."

Jim Hunt grew up in Wilson, thirty miles east of Raleigh, and some of his earliest memories involved his father peeling potatoes at their boarding house while listening to N. C. State sporting events on the radio. He was a boy of twelve in December 1949 when he accompanied his Wolfpack-obsessed father to the first basketball game ever played in Reynolds Coliseum. The two soon became regulars at the Dixie Classics, and in 1955 Hunt made the logical choice—N. C. State—when it was time to select a college. In a touch of foreshadowing, he spent two years as the NCSU student body president, two decades before he was first elected governor of North Carolina. He governed the state from 1977 to 1985 and again from 1993 to 2001, becoming the longest-serving governor in North Carolina's history. As a young aspiring leader, one of his role models was the coach who was inspiring so much passion for basketball on his campus.

"He was larger than life then," Hunt said of Case. "He brought big-time basketball here. Everett Case was not seen a lot, but we heard a lot about him. We knew what a terrific basketball coach he was. He was the king of coaches. He had this concept of what could be, this vision of what could be here in North Carolina. He had a pretty big view of where the best basketball was being played, and when he came here he knew how to bring the best basketball here."

Never was Hunt's devotion to the holiday tournament tested more severely than in 1959, when he was a first-year law student at the University of North Carolina and his wife Carolyn was overdue with their first child. The baby was expected in the middle of December, but it was now December 30, the day of the final rounds of that year's Classic, and her labor was finally getting underway. Hunt drove Carolyn to Rex

Hospital in Raleigh, got her checked in, gave her a kiss, and headed back to Reynolds to catch the basketball games. He checked in by pay phone periodically, learned that her labor was moving slowly, and stayed at the arena through the championship game. After the final buzzer sounded, Hunt lost no time getting back to Rex Hospital, and he made it in time to see his oldest daughter enter the world early in the morning of December 31. "Finally, after a long day's basketball, with me seeing every minute of it, our first child was born," he said.

"The event brought in all the leaders of North Carolina and the great sports fans of this state," Hunt observed. "The quality of the teams and the play was of the highest order. The excitement and the cheering of the fans and getting into the spirit of it was as great as any event I've ever attended, of any kind, including political conventions. It was a time when you really found out who was best. It was an intense environment."

Hunt wasn't the only future North Carolina dignitary who became a regular Dixie Classic spectator. William Friday was in his early thirties and on the rise in higher education, serving at that time as the assistant to Gordon Gray, who was the president of the Consolidated University of North Carolina. Gray was prone to flu and other sickness, Friday said, and he was convinced that the smoke and crowds at Reynolds would be harmful to him, so he enlisted Friday to escort his four sons to every round of the Dixie Classic. Only a few years later, Friday would wield more influence over the Dixie Classic than any player or coach ever did.

As college basketball in the South moved into the spotlight and the Dixie Classic became the not-to-miss event of the holiday season, the nation's professional basketball leagues were struggling to find their way. The NBA had been in existence since 1946. Even though players only made an average of $5,000 a year with no pension and no benefits, it was still a popular destination for talented players who were not quite ready to put the basketball down. One player who made the jump was former Duke standout Dick Groat, who was drafted by the Fort Wayne Pistons in 1952 and played just twenty-six games for the team in the spring of 1953 while he earned the credits he needed to graduate from Duke. After that season Groat, who had also been drafted by the Pittsburgh Pirates to play baseball, served for two years in the Korean War, and when he returned the Pirates owner told him he had to focus solely on baseball. A big, athletic pivotman from New York, Jack Molinas, came to the Pistons later in 1953, while Groat was in Korea. Molinas, the hotshot from Columbia whose coach had bragged on him during the 1951 Dixie Classic, rented space in the house Groat had secured in Fort Wayne.

Groat and Molinas never played together for the Pistons, however, because Molinas did not even last his rookie season. In January of 1954 he was accused of fixing games in which he played, and NBA commissioner Maurice Podoloff demanded his resignation. Back from the war the next year, Groat renewed a major-league baseball career that lasted fifteen years, moving on as Molinas waged a battle to get reinstated by the NBA and continued to cultivate long-held relationships with the New York gamblers and bookmakers who watched basketball results with more than just a fan's interest.

II
ZENITH
1954–1959

Six

N. C. State seemed to be at the end of its Dixie Classic reign. Now that Duke owned a trophy, the other Big Four rivals and the out-of-state interlopers became even more focused on getting their hands on one. Each December brought a larger dose of Classic enthusiasm, as fans fixated on finding tickets and college basketball coaches jockeyed for an invitation. It was clear by the mid-fifties that inclusion in the Dixie Classic field was a stamp of excellence on a basketball program, even though it would be a few more years before the most memorable Classic, the one against which all others would one day be measured.

Bucky Waters played for the Wolfpack during those years and later coached at Duke and West Virginia, but he was a Camden, New Jersey, native who grew up thinking that Madison Square Garden and the Palestra were the centers of the basketball world. After his southern relocation, he noticed a shift in the landscape, one driven by Everett Case and the national impact of his Dixie Classic. "It got the reputation of, 'If you've really arrived, you'll be invited to the Dixie Classic,'" Waters said.

At the annual Tip-Off Club luncheon for tournament coaches and officials in 1954, UNC coach Frank McGuire warned his visiting colleagues about NCSU's Dixie Classic hospitality. The host team is all warmth and accommodation before the tournament begins, he observed, but when the first ball is tipped they are bent on humiliating their guests. "They make you feel at home early in the morning and late at night, but when the game starts over at the Coliseum, all hell breaks loose."

Several of the 1954 contenders had already established themselves as national powerhouses. Southern California came to Raleigh determined to find redemption from its 1951 Classic appearance, when they arrived as a favorite and then fell in the first round to Carolina. They drew the Tar Heels again on the first day, and the Trojans were again favored to win, but history repeated itself as UNC prevailed 67–58 behind the stellar shooting of sophomore Lennie Rosenbluth. "Our kids just couldn't shoot," USC coach Forrest Twogood told reporters afterwards. "Otherwise, we played a good game."

The other visiting teams that posed major threats in 1954 were West Virginia, with two-time All-American "Hot Rod" Hundley; and Minnesota, a top Big Ten team featuring a sharpshooting guard named Dick Garmaker and Bill Simonovich, an intimidating six eleven forward who even dwarfed six six Wake Forest center Dickie Hemric. "I remember the guy," Hemrick said. "His hands were so big, and he could grip a Coca-Cola bottle, he could basically grip it from the base to the neck and conceal it."

Hundley, known for his fancy ball handling, "did every magical trick with the ball except that of turning it into a rabbit, but he couldn't score," against Duke in the first round, according to the *News and Observer*. He only managed six points, and the defending Classic champions lived to fight another day. It was Minnesota that truly made its presence known in the Coliseum, toppling first Wake Forest, then Duke en route to a final with N. C. State. The team from the icy North came just seconds from taking home the championship, but sophomore Wolfpack guard John Maglio flipped in a desperation shot with nine seconds left on the clock for an 85–84 win and NCSU's return to the top.

After coming less than ten seconds from making history as the first out-of-state team to win the Classic, Minnesota returned in 1955 to try again, becoming the only visiting squad to make consecutive trips to the event. And even though the Golden Gophers had proven they could be a threat, the records of the teams in the 1955 field illustrated how routine basketball excellence was becoming within North Carolina. Minnesota arrived in Raleigh 3–2, and the other three visitors brought similar or worse records—Oregon State was 3–4, Villanova was 3–2, and Wyoming was 1–7. The Big Four, however, came in with only one imperfect mark among them. Duke was 6–0, N. C. State was 8–0, North Carolina was 5–0, and Wake Forest was 5–3, having lost their first three and arrived at the tournament on a hot streak after winning the Carrousel tournament in Charlotte.

The stage seemed perfectly set for a Tar Heel State sweep, as Dick Herbert wrote on opening day: "Making all allowances, the seventh Dixie Classic shapes up as a show with the Big Four teams in the lead roles." And that's exactly what the first day of play brought—victories by all four local teams—and a second day that had every fan unlucky enough to lack a ticket playing all the angles in a desperate effort to obtain one. It was the first time every Tobacco Road team had prevailed in the opening round. While Everett Case declared his Wolfpack's performance in a 59–54 victory over Oregon State the worst he had ever seen from one of his NCSU teams, the messy win still provided the ultimate grudge match—a second-round tilt with hated rival Wake Forest.

Fueled by 20 points from junior Cliff Hafer, N. C. State shook off its early tournament lethargy to dispatch Wake Forest 70–58, and Carolina likewise beat Duke 74–64 to set up the first N. C. State-North Carolina final in Dixie Classic history. The Tar Heels were sniffing their first championship, but a Wolfpack team that many considered one of the best in history hit on all cylinders in the New Year's Eve showdown and won handily by a score of 82–60 for their sixth Classic title. According to Dick Herbert, "Coach Everett Case's classy crew settled for this time the question of neighborhood supremacy by outplaying the previously undefeated Tar Heels all of the way and in every phase of play."

Case was effusive in his praise of his 11–0 squad, who had made the march to the top of the field look so easy that UNC coach Frank McGuire thanked Case afterward for putting in his subs when he could have easily run up the score. "It's the best State team I've seen," McGuire said. "They were simply terrific." Guards Vic Molodet and John Maglio made up one of the best backcourt tandems in the nation, and Ronnie Shavlik, the MVP of both the '54 and '55 Dixie Classics, was looking like a world-beater. Just after the Dixie Classic, national polls put the Wolfpack at number two, just behind San Francisco with its talented center Bill Russell.

The Wolfpack eventually picked up three losses, but they were still viewed as the best in the ACC even when Hafer was released from the team for honor code violations in February and Shavlik broke his wrist in the final game of the regular season the following month. Expected to miss the rest of the season, Shavlik's value to the team was so high that he competed in a cast in the ACC Tournament and the NCAA Tournament, earning so much national attention for his courage that he appeared on the *Perry Como Show* that spring.

Shavlik continued to amaze in the Wolfpack's first-round NCAA tournament game, which was played against Canisius at Madison Square Garden, an arena that had long vexed Case's teams. Shavlik finished with 25 points and 17 rebounds, prompting Canisius coach Joe Curran to say, "I would hate to see Shavlik with two arms." The game was a marathon that extended to four overtimes—still a record for playoff games—but only ended in exhaustion and disappointment for N. C. State. With fourteen seconds left in the fourth extra period, the Wolfpack held a one-point lead, but Maglio missed a key free throw and Frank Corcoran, a Canisius substitute who had averaged less than a point a game during the regular season, hit a last-second basket to seal the win.

To his dying day, Case would name the Canisius game as his single most devastating loss. The team that had started the season with such boundless promise and had overcome even a star player's broken wrist fell short in the season that was probably Case's best hope for a national championship. And the sting was undoubtedly sharpened by the things that would threaten to cripple his team just a few months later and the good fortune that would soon come to his rival down the road.

By 1955, Everett Case was preparing for his tenth season at the helm of the Wolfpack, and in that decade he had been a positive presence, a coach who seemed allergic to failure with the motivational skills to build winning teams and the loyalty to convince State fans that he was theirs for good. But by the mid-fifties, talk of television coverage was widening the lens trained on college basketball, and with a higher profile came greater scrutiny. Suddenly coaches who had always gotten by doing things their own way were being pressed for answers—and the NCAA was showing a willingness to punish the programs whose practices were beyond the pale.

Case first aroused suspicion for his recruitment of Shavlik, a high school phenomenon from Denver who became one of the Wolfpack's first true superstars. The NCAA accused Case of impropriety for paying the travel expenses of a prospect in 1953, and though never named, that player was believed to be Ronnie Shavlik. Case's pursuit of a player from the Rockies was unusual in an era when top coaches seemed like salesmen who stuck strictly to their territories: Case recruited in Indiana and New Jersey, McGuire in New York, Duke coach Hal Bradley in Philadelphia. Shavlik became a Wolfpack legend, an All-American, and a two-time Dixie Classic MVP (his grandson and namesake, Ronald Shavlik Randolph, would play at Duke and in the NBA), but the NCAA made Case pay for those recruiting violations by banning N. C. State from participation in the 1955 NCAA Tournament.

The second black mark on Case's otherwise pristine reputation resulted from another unusual recruiting destination—Minden, Louisiana. Jackie Moreland, a talented and versatile big man, had attracted the attention of every major college coach in the country, and Case was determined to get him for the Wolfpack. Moreland signed with N. C. State in 1956 and created an immediate sensation on the freshman team, scoring 30 in a game in which he sat out the final ten minutes.

It was the only game Moreland would ever play in an N. C. State uniform. After that game, the NCAA announced that Case and his staff had illegally recruited Moreland, and as a result the entire N. C. State athletic program was put on probation for four years. The punishment was unusually harsh, the NCAA explained, because of N. C. State's earlier infraction and because of the overwhelming evidence in the Moreland case, which included the following allegations: Moreland was promised $200 a year for clothing and an annual gift of $1,000, and his girlfriend was promised an expense-paid trip to Raleigh for Thanksgiving and a seven-year college and medical school education. Because of the violations, Moreland was asked to leave N. C. State, and Wolfpack teams in all sports were banned from NCAA championships and postseason events. It was a sizable bump in the road for Case, especially since he had his sights set on a national title. But it did little to diminish his image in the eyes of the Wolfpack faithful, and he denied all of the charges except one involving $80 given to Moreland for transportation to Raleigh.

"If you're going to convict schools on charges like these, I can tell you that there wouldn't be very many left to play basketball or anything," Case said at the time. "They are getting mighty thin, splitting hairs, grasping at technicalities."

N. C. State wasn't the only Big Four program arousing suspicion for its recruiting practices in those days. As Case and his team took their lumps, whispers continued to circulate about Frank McGuire and his network of friends and associates in New York City, where his "Underground Railroad" offered a steady supply of Big Apple talent. *Sports Illustrated* ran an article in which two McGuire cronies admitted to receiving money from McGuire for their recruiting help, but the UNC coach consistently denied the accusations. However he obtained his players, though, the New York connection would prove to be quite fruitful for McGuire as the 1956–57 season dawned.

As the season opened in Chapel Hill McGuire had some things to celebrate, but equal cause for concern. The team picture that December, as they won eight straight en route to the 1956 Dixie Classic, bore only a passing resemblance to the photo they would take in March. Guard Harvey Salz dropped out of school in December, senior Tony Radovich was only eligible to play during the fall semester, and by February both six foot eleven center Bill Hathaway and Stan Groll would be disqualified from play for academic reasons. McGuire even had to go out and find six foot six center Bob Young, who had struggled with academic ineligibility as an underclassman, and bring him back on to get his roster to ten.

Still, the Tar Heels had star junior Lennie Rosenbluth, who would be the target of every opposing defense, and Rosenbluth was aided by fellow New Yorkers Pete Brennan, Joe Quigg, Bob Cunningham, and Tommy Kearns. Rosenbluth came out like a man on fire in the first round of the Dixie Classic that year, scoring 36 points to help his team dominate Utah 97–76. The next day looked similar, except this time Rosenbluth unleashed on his neighbors at Duke, scoring 32 points to defeat the Blue Devils 87–71. Meanwhile, Wake Forest was finding its own redemption with a second-round victory over N. C. State, the first time they had beat the Wolfpack since the 1953 Dixie Classic.

For the second consecutive year, the Big Four teams had dominated the winner's bracket, but this final would pit

Carolina against Wake Forest. Mindful of McGuire's chief offensive weapon, WFU coach Murray Greason came in with a defensive game plan to shut off Rosenbluth's prolific scoring. The plan worked—Rosenbluth scored only 18 points, and 12 of those came at the free-throw line—but Cunningham and Brennan, with 13 and 11 points, contributed enough to keep the Tar Heels in front for virtually the entire evening and give them a 63–55 win for their first Dixie Classic trophy.

It was an impressive display, prompting a *Time* magazine writer to report, "McGuire's troops moved the ball with such polished skill and shot with such consistent effect that they more than backed up his boast that Carolina teams rank with the best collegiate teams around." But if a national magazine or a local sportswriter had used any newsprint to speculate on the possibility of the Tar Heels going unbeaten throughout the entire season, they would have faced derision from fans, players, and fellow reporters. Such a prediction would have been viewed as overly dramatic and completely ungrounded in reality. Even Frank McGuire, as his team kept accumulating wins early in 1957, declared, "There's no such thing as an undefeated season in basketball."

His own team proved him wrong. That Dixie Classic title helped set the pace for the unlikeliest of scenarios: a Tar Heel squad that ran the table for a 32–0 record that ended with a victory over Wilt Chamberlain and Kansas in the NCAA Tournament. North Carolina, the team that just four years earlier had been mired in a fifteen-game losing streak to N. C. State, had captured the country's imagination with a perfect season and a national championship. It was an accomplishment that could be clearly traced to Case's influence on the basketball culture in the state, but that was little comfort to a Wolfpack program that had showed every sign of beating the other Big Four teams to the top of the college basketball mountain.

Tar Heel boosters rewarded McGuire with a brand-new blue and white Cadillac, and his bosses gave him a raise and a new five-year contract. And every young boy in the vicinity who did not already have a basketball goal outside started to ask his parents for one, inspired by the history making Tar Heels. The team's singular impact on fans was intensified by a brand-new development that would later wield a huge influence on the way the sport was distributed, funded, and received: the decision to broadcast college games on television.

It's tough to imagine in an era where the only holiday tournaments are made-for-TV events like the Maui Invitational, but in the 1950s basketball purists were hesitant about the introduction of broadcast coverage because they worried that television would erode attendance in the arenas. McGuire, though, saw the handwriting on the wall and allowed a 1955 Carolina-Wake Forest game to be broadcast on a Chapel Hill public station as an experiment. That broadcast was little more than a lark, but as the 1957 UNC squad kept winning, a Philadelphia producer named C. D. Chesley saw a revolutionary opportunity and put together a network of North Carolina stations to air two of the Final Four games that year.

The NCAA final that year between Kansas and North Carolina on March 23, 1957, was broadcast throughout the state, with the signal transmitted through phone lines Chesley had hastily rented for that purpose. It was a late-evening tip-off and Chesley wondered if anyone would really stay up to tune in. The next day, he told the Greensboro *Daily News*, it seemed that most of North Carolina had watched the game. "We got letters from fans two years later thanking us for televising that one game against Kansas," he reflected years afterward.

Television coverage would eventually infiltrate all parts of the big-time college game, but even as fans relived the highlights of Chamberlain's matchup with Lennie Rosenbluth and became instant North Carolina adherents, the Dixie Classic continued as it always had—a traditional tournament run for the sole benefit of the people in the stands. Even without television cameras, the media presence at the Classic was overwhelming. It was the golden age of newspapers, and sportswriters from every daily in North Carolina and many from outside the state started writing N. C. State's sports information director in the fall requesting press passes and the complimentary tickets that were generally bestowed on the media during those years.

In one such request, for the 1953 Classic, Frankie Patterson, sports editor of the *Daily Independent* in Kannapolis, captured the pre-tournament mood in a letter to NCSU sports information director Ed Story: "Things are humming around here concerning the big Dixie Cage Classic later this month and the requests about tickets and other information has been heavy," Patterson wrote. "I believe the attendance from around here should be fine. I plan to witness all of the event and feel sure that it will be the best in history. The competition should be keen."

The media ticket list for the 1956 Dixie Classic, handwritten on a legal pad, includes allotments for thirty-three different newspapers and nine radio stations. The hosts were generous to their reporter friends, especially those in their backyard: The 1955 ticket list indicates that Raleigh *News and Observer* sports editor Dick Herbert, one of the original masterminds of the Dixie Classic, would receive five working press passes, six complimentary tickets, five wives' tickets, two photo passes, and five parking passes for Herbert and his staff.

Of course, sportswriting was an old boys network in that era, a fact that is illustrated vividly in Dixie Classic correspondence. One 1960 letter from the NCSU athletic department to the media concerns the abuse of "wives' tickets," a moniker which assumed only male writers would be in attendance. Sportswriters who received wives' tickets and did not plan on bringing their wives had apparently been giving them to younger family members or selling them to friends, a practice expressly forbidden. "The biggest abuse of the entire tournament revolves around wives' row tickets," the notice read. "This is a privilege which should be guarded carefully. Only twenty-five of these tickets are made available, and, of course, cannot accommodate everyone."

Visiting media were entertained during their stay and many of those gatherings were strictly men-only. Another athletic department policy from the late fifties concerned two separate Reynolds Coliseum hospitality rooms, one for men and one for women, as well as the hospitality room at the Sir Walter Raleigh Hotel downtown, which was open nightly for cocktails. "Women are invited to the Saturday night party ONLY," the letter said of the New Year's Eve party at the Sir Walter, scheduled for 11:00 P.M. to 1:00 A.M. after the final Classic game.

Earmarks of the Dixie Classic's surging popularity were everywhere, from crowded conditions on media row to desperate quests for tickets and the annual rash of "Dixie Classic" specials at Raleigh stores and restaurants. Ensconced in the coliseum that loomed as the icon of his influence on NCSU and the region, Everett Case was unflagging in his efforts to keep the Classic at the top of the tournament heap. And no task was more vital in that quest than the annual recruitment of visiting teams. Big Four fans would always show up, but to be the best Case had to bring in the best competition, schools that were making a national splash and might have the chops to carry a Dixie Classic championship trophy across state lines.

Coincidentally, the player that would soon give Case's event the biggest boost it ever enjoyed shared his Indiana basketball heritage. Oscar Robertson's family was originally from Tennessee, but when he was four years old they moved to Indianapolis, a city that was as highly segregated as any in the South during those years. Growing up in the black community of Indianapolis, Robertson soon became a regular at the vacant dirt lots near his house, courts that someone nicknamed "The Dust Bowl." Before long his ball handling and shooting were attracting attention, and in 1955 and 1956 he led Crispus Attucks High School to two consecutive state titles—the first African-American high school to tread that hallowed Indiana ground.

Robertson was certainly on Case's radar, even though it would be almost another decade before any ACC school would entertain the idea of integrating its basketball team. So Case did the next best thing to recruiting Robertson: He invited him to play in the Dixie Classic. Not long after Robertson enrolled at his chosen school, the University of Cincinnati, in the fall of 1956, Case had already secured a commitment from Bearcats coach George Smith to play in the 1958 Classic.

The same year that Robertson began his college career, a late bloomer named Johnny Green was playing for the freshman team at Michigan State. Green was still barely six feet tall, a Korean War veteran working at a junkyard, when he unexpectedly grew to six foot five inches after his twentieth birthday. He enrolled at Michigan State, where he set Big Ten scoring and rebounding records and made the Spartans an immediate national threat. Shortly after he secured Robertson and Cincinnati, Case made another phone call, to MSU coach Forddy Anderson, and invited "Jumpin' Johnny Green" and his squad to join Cincinnati at the 1958 Classic, which would mark the tenth anniversary of the tournament. By boldly assembling the greatest field in the event's history, Case had guaranteed that the 1958 milestone Dixie Classic would be the most memorable one yet.

Seven

Most Division I basketball coaches were quick to accept an invitation to play in the prestigious Dixie Classic, but warm southern hospitality was not extended to all potential competitors in the tournament's early years. Athletic director Leo Harris of the University of Oregon gauged the climate to be unfriendly enough that he declined to bring his team to the 1950 Classic.

The Ducks' roster featured a black player named Mel Streeter that season, and after Everett Case invited them to join the Dixie Classic field N. C. State chancellor Roy Clogston wrote Harris a letter expressing his belief that the experience would be much better for Oregon if they made the trip without Streeter. "I seriously doubt if it would be wise for us to be the first to play a colored athlete," Clogston wrote. Having no wish to re-segregate a team that had been integrated, Harris declined.

Collegiate basketball squads like Rutgers, Nebraska, and Penn State had welcomed black players before World War I, and the Big Ten was officially integrated in 1945 with Richard Culbertson at the University of Iowa. But it was a trend that stopped short at the Mason-Dixon line. And southern athletic directors did not just concern themselves with the racial makeup of their own teams; for decades, major college sports teams in the South were intentional about keeping their opponents segregated as well. In some cases the opposing coach was even asked to sign a contract stating that he would either

leave his black players at home or keep them on the bench.
Some, like Harris, refused to capitulate on that condition.
Penn State agreed to come to the inaugural Dixie Classic in
1949 without Hardy Williams, who had become that school's
first African-American basketball player the previous year.

Penn State won its first two Classic games and lost in the final to N. C. State. The Nittany Lions could have used Williams;
Penn only had eight men on its roster that evening, and two
starters—Lou Lamie and Marty Costa—fouled out during the
second half. Williams, who years later went on to serve in the
Pennsylvania state senate, paved the way for Penn State All-
American Jessie Arnelle.

With the precedent thus established, N. C. State administrators continued to politely ask teams to travel to Raleigh
with whites only, but in 1953 they faced a situation that was
beyond their control. NCSU had won the right to host the NCAA
Eastern Regional at Reynolds Coliseum, and one of the competing teams was Penn State, with Arnelle already a star as
a freshman. Arnelle played brilliantly and the game drew no
controversy, prompting a different kind of letter from Clogston
to Temple University athletic director Josh Cody in 1954.

"Your colored boys will be treated just the same as anyone
else," Clogston wrote to Cody. "Arnelle of Penn State played
here in our Coliseum, and he received the greatest ovation I
have ever seen given any athlete in the William Neal Reynolds
Coliseum."

Later in 1953 Seton Hall came to the Dixie Classic, and
Frank Minaya, an African-American center, made the trip with
the Pirates. But his name is listed in none of the box scores
from the tournament, and Greensboro *Daily News* writer
Irwin Smallwood confirmed Minaya's non-participation with
this item in his column on the final day of the event: "Seton
Hall beat Tulane in a great basketball exhibition, when the
scrubs of the two teams remained on the Coliseum floor for

almost an hour in a friendly scrimmage game. Seton Hall's big Negro, who didn't get in the regular game, was a welcome participant."

Four years later, another Seton Hall player made history as the first African-American to play in a regular Dixie Classic game. Seth Hicks was a junior forward who was usually a steady scorer for the Pirates, but he only converted one basket against Duke in the 1957 opening round, and an injury he incurred in that game forced him to sit out the next two games. Still, he made the trip to Raleigh, and no controversy was reported surrounding his visit.

These were baby steps toward integration in the college game—conceding that Big Four fans could be prevailed upon to watch a team with black players—and in the mid-fifties the notion that any major North Carolina university would actually recruit an African-American athlete seemed light years away. Privately, though, Everett Case was considering it.

In some regards Case's home state of Indiana was as racially divided as any part of the South. Oscar Robertson remembers that after his Crispus Attucks team won the state title, city officials refused to let the team drive on the traditional champions' parade route through downtown, instead redirecting them to the black part of town. It came out later that the mayor was afraid that if the Attucks team celebrated in the center of town (as every previous winning team had) the city ran the risk of a riot.

But Indiana basketball did topple some barriers, and in one instance the revolutionary was none other than legendary college coach John Wooden. Before he led his UCLA teams to an unrivaled ten national titles in the sixties and seventies, Wooden coached at Indiana State in the mid-forties, and in 1947 he refused an invitation for his team to play in the National Association of Intercollegiate Basketball (NAIB) National Tournament, the most prestigious postseason event

for small colleges, because the tournament had a policy banning African-American participants and Wooden's team featured Clarence Walker, a black player. The following year
tournament organizers integrated the event, and Wooden allowed his team to compete.

Case was undoubtedly influenced by the changes in
Indiana and even by the reports he was hearing from African-
American colleges like North Carolina Central in nearby
Durham, where coach John McLendon was running the fast-
break offense—and had been since 1939, years before Case arrived in North Carolina. McLendon's advisor when he was a
student at the University of Kansas was none other than James
Naismith himself, and McLendon's complex offensive strategy
and structured practice philosophy unleashed an offensive attack that led his Eagles to break national scoring records and
draw larger and larger crowds to its arena. All-white squads
from large universities were getting credit for advancing the
game in the state, but players at black high schools and colleges were playing head-turning basketball themselves, and
not even segregation could keep the word from reaching a
basketball visionary like Case.

In 1956, Case summoned Bob Kennel to his office. Kennel
was a three-sport athlete from New Bern, North Carolina,
who had played on the NCSU freshman basketball team and
then quit to focus on just baseball and football. The subject of
the meeting was Walt Bellamy, a talented six foot eleven post
player who was finishing his high school career in Kennel's
hometown. Both Kennel and Bellamy were great young players in New Bern, but athletic competition was divided along
racial lines at every level in those days, so they never had the
chance to play against each other. Kennel had heard that there
was a great player at J. T. Barber High, but he did not even
know his name until Case approached him. Bellamy had been
recruited by a number of northern programs and had already

committed to the University of Indiana, but Case wondered if he should try to convince him to stay close to home and be a part of Wolfpack history.

Happy to do a favor for Coach Case, Kennel called his father, a foot carrier for the post office who was assigned to the part of town where most of the African-Americans lived. His father knew Bellamy, and he arranged a meeting between Kennel, Bellamy, Bellamy's father, and his high school coach. Bellamy's father did most of the talking, and he told Kennel that they still felt Indiana was the right place for him. When Kennel told Case that they wouldn't get their man, Case said, "It's probably just as well. I'm not sure he's a good enough ballplayer to be the one who makes the break."

Case's assessment proved uncharacteristically wrong. Bellamy went on to become a two-time All-American, widely considered to be the best center in Indiana history. He also excelled in a fourteen-year NBA career that culminated with his selection to the Naismith Basketball Hall of Fame in 1993. One of Bellamy's basketball highlights came in 1960, when he helped the U. S. Olympic Team win the gold medal at the Rome Games with teammate Oscar Robertson, a guard whose ball handling and athleticism were already becoming the stuff of legend.

Jesse Arnelle had commanded a standing ovation and a handful of other African-American players had competed in large southern arenas, but from 1949 to 1957 the Dixie Classic had remained the domain of white fans and athletes. And because Robertson from Cincinnati and Johnny Green from Michigan State were both All-Americans on top-ranked teams, the hype leading up to the 1958 Classic was unrivaled. Cincinnati was number one in the nation, Michigan State was number four, North Carolina was number five, and N. C. State was ranked number six. Three of the teams were undefeated, and State had lost just one game. It may have been a civil rights accomplishment, but most of the fans in the Big Four were more focused on basketball glory than social progress in late 1958.

As the faithful clamored for tickets and media from all over vied for seats on press row, the Classic organizers were occupied with normal logistical matters like food and lodging for the participating teams. But because of Cincinnati and Michigan State's inclusion in the field, those issues were suddenly far from routine. Tournament director Willis Casey wrote to authorities at both schools offering to arrange separate accommodations for Green and teammate Horace Walker, and Robertson and his teammate John Bryant, since the Sir Walter Raleigh Hotel was not open to blacks. As Robertson wrote years later in his autobiography, *The Big O: My Life, My Times, My Game*, it would have been an ideal time for his alma mater to take a stand.

"Until my dying day, I will believe that all my school would have had to do was tell North Carolina State and the tournament planners, 'If Oscar Robertson and John Bryant can't stay at the hotel in downtown Raleigh, we're not going to play.' If they had shown some backbone and said that, I expect that everything else would have taken care of itself. But they did not. Instead, a conscious choice was made in the other direction."

As the player who broke the color barrier at Cincinnati, the separate housing question was a drill he had been run through before, most dramatically on a road trip to Houston in early 1958. The Bearcats team was staying in the landmark Shamrock Hilton Hotel southwest of downtown, and the players were trying to get some rest in preparation for the next day's game against the University of Houston when a phone call from the hotel manager roused Cincinnati coach George Smith at midnight. The manager told Smith that he had to get Robertson out of the Shamrock at once.

"I called Harry Faulk, the athletic director at Houston, and asked him what the hell was going on," Smith recalled

Across North Carolina young boys like this Duke fan dreamed of getting their hands on Dixie Classic tickets, often in their stockings on Christmas morning.

Reynolds Coliseum in April of 1950, five months after hosting its first basketball game. N.C. State officials made sure the arena had a door large enough for elephants to pass through so that circuses could be held there.

Frank McGuire, who took the head coaching job at North Carolina in 1952, was known for his dapper dressing and his connections with people on the right and the wrong sides of the law in his native New York City.

Bones McKinney's antics on the sideline were legendary during Dixie Classics. Said one visiting player: "Bones was a wild man."

Murray Greason goofs with Stan Najway (*left*) and Jack Mueller. Greason led the Wake Forest team for twenty-four years, and was known as a calm presence on the bench, in sharp contrast to his animated assistant Bones McKinney.

(Top) Columbia went 1–2 in the 1951 Classic. Later, their head coach lamented the absence of star forward Jack Molinas, who was under suspension because of a disciplinary issue but would later figure prominently in the scandal that toppled the Classic.

(Above) The N.C. State team react to a good play at the 1951 Classic. The Wolfpack took the first four championship trophies at their signature tournament.

(Left) 1950 Dixie Classic Queen Sarah French presents Sammy Ranzino with his MVP trophy. Ranzino scored 33 points against Rhode Island in the first round.

Duke player Junior Morgan puts in a basket against Navy in the final game of the 1953 Dixie Classic. The Blue Devils surprised observers by winning the tournament that year for what would be their only Dixie Classic title.

After winning the 1953 Classic, Duke head coach Hal Bradley got to cut down the last strand of the Reynolds net, following a tradition brought from Indiana by Everett Case.

In the second round of the 1953 tournament, Navy became the first team to ever beat N. C. State in the Classic.

Griffin's Barbecue of Goldsboro sold plates to hungry fans in the Reynolds Coliseum basement between the afternoon and evening sessions of the Classic.

The Dixie Classic Queen traditionally handed out the trophies to the MVP and the winning team, but a few of those presentations led to surprisingly bold kisses on the Reynolds Coliseum floor. 1953 queen Pat Gibson kisses Rudy D'Emilio, the MVP from Duke.

A year after winning the 1956 Dixie Classic, the North Carolina Tar Heels won another one, defeating N.C. State 39–30 for the 1957 trophy.

Cincinnati's Oscar Robertson beats back five Deacon defenders to get to the basket. Robertson was the most celebrated player ever to play in the Dixie Classic. The Reynolds Coliseum crowd got its first look at his athleticism in this match against Wake Forest.

Robertson taking a breather between games with teammates Mike Mendenhall and Mel Landfried (24).

In one of the most discussed incidents in Classic history, Robertson and Wake Forest's Dave Budd got into a scuffle after getting tangled up under the basket. Robertson later said the spat was just a product of physical basketball.

Robertson jumps over North Carolina's Dick Kepley in the consolation final of the 1958 Classic.

After defeating UNC in the semifinal, Michigan State was confident of its chances to become the first Classic champion from outside North Carolina. Johnny Green, center, and teammates Horace Walker and Bob Anderegg do a little gloating after the UNC victory.

In a tournament full of intense battles, the 1958 final between N.C. State and Michigan State was the perfect capper. John Richter of the Wolfpack defends fan favorite Johnny Green en route to N.C. State's seventh and final Classic title.

Michigan State's Horace Walker, who was limited in the championship by an injured ankle, still launches a shot against the Wolfpack, while Johnny Green shows off his own aeronautics to the left.

Everett Case's relationship with his players went so deep that he divided a large portion of his estate among former Wolfpack athletes. After his team battled to victory in the hard-fought 1958 Dixie Classic, he rides off the court on the team's shoulders.

N.C. State's John Richter *(left)* and Lou Pucillo *(right)*, known as "Mutt and Jeff" for their contrasting heights and friendship on and off the court, are jubilant after their team's 1958 Classic win.

(*Above*) In 1959, NCSU stumbled early in the Classic against Dayton, losing a game which two Wolfpack players later admitted to fixing. Everett Case talks strategy with his team, including point-shaver Anton Muehlbauer (52).

(*Right*) Stan Niewierowski (42) and Don Gallagher (44) fight for control of the ball in the 1959 Classic. In court testimony two years later, both men confessed to shaving points in the Wolfpack's game against Dayton, which their team lost 36–32.

Sophomore Billy Packer (34) scores a lay-up against Holy Cross in the first round of the 1959 Dixie Classic.

The 1959 Classic was the second tournament that ended with North Carolina and Wake Forest meeting in the final, but this time Wake Forest prevailed. Battles in the post like this one defined the game, which the Deacons won 53–50.

Billy Packer, who went on to become the lead college basketball analyst for CBS and NBC for thirty-six years, was named the MVP of the 1959 Dixie Classic, receiving his trophy from Queen Susan Woodall.

(Above) The Wake Forest team celebrates its 1959 championship. Billy Packer is on the lower left, with coach Bones McKinney to his right.

(Below, left) The MVP of the 1960 Classic, UNC's Doug Moe, with Queen Delia Chamberlin. Moe left UNC a few months after this photo was taken because of a connection with the point-shaving scandal, but while he accepted $75 for travel he never fixed any games.

(Below, right) North Carolina player York Larese gets a look at the 1960 program.

Dixie Classic contests between Duke and North Carolina, like this championship game in 1960, helped spark a rivalry that many consider the greatest in college basketball.

Typical attire for the Reynolds Coliseum crowd at the Dixie Classic was a coat and tie for the men and dresses and hats for the ladies.

Bones McKinney is grilled by the press at the 1960 Classic. Held in the heyday of the sports newspaperman, the Dixie Classic featured dozens of print reporters from all over the Southeast.

UNC head coach Frank McGuire (*right*) and his young assistant Dean Smith talk through strategy with their players at the 1960 tournament. The Tar Heels went on to win the final Dixie Classic championship.

Everett Case coaching in the final Dixie Classic. Bob Kennel, who played briefly for Case, observed, "The Dixie Classic, it was just Everett Case, ahead of everybody and everything."

William Friday, president of the Consolidated University of North Carolina, which included N. C. State, UNC, and the University of North Carolina at Greensboro, around the time of the Classic's cancellation.

The front *(above)* and inside *(below)* of Case's Christmas card the year after the Dixie Classic was cancelled.

for an interviewer years later. "He told me they were expecting Oscar at [Texas] Southern University for the night. The thought crossed my mind to pull the whole team out of the hotel and forfeit tomorrow's game and get on the next plane back to Cincinnati."

Instead, Smith walked down the hall and knocked on Robertson's door. The Texas Southern coach was also rousted out of bed to find a spare dorm room for Robertson, who just weeks earlier had set a Madison Square Garden scoring record with 56 points in a game against Seton Hall. Smith arranged for transportation, and Robertson soon found himself in a small dorm room on a bunk bed at the historically black Texas Southern, miles away from the rest of his team.

"As much as it bothered me that the hotel wouldn't let me stay there, I was just as bothered at being the only person who had to move," Robertson said in his biography. "All this talk about being a team and winning and losing together, staying together and doing things together—as a team. 'What just happened?' I asked myself. I had momentarily forgotten this was America."

On that same road trip, the team visited Denton, Texas, to play against North Texas State. The arena was packed with North Texas fans, and from the very beginning the spectators shouted racial slurs at Robertson and threw food and programs at him from the stands. Robertson, heckled throughout the contest, only scored 13 points. When the team returned to Cincinnati, he went to Coach Smith's office and told him that if he was made to stay separately from his team again, he would quit the team. "From that day forward," he said, "I grew up fast."

Robertson was a junior averaging 38.8 points a game when his Bearcats squad arrived in Raleigh on Sunday, December 28. As a sophomore, he had led the nation in scoring with an average of 35.14 points a game. His future included both Olympic triumph and a fourteen-year NBA career in which he became

the top-scoring guard in history. He was also the only professional player ever to average a triple-double (double-digit totals in scoring, rebounds, and assists) over an entire season. In
2000 he was named the Player of the Century by the National
Association of Basketball Coaches. Yet as his visit to the Dixie
Classic neared, Everett Case had to turn to a college fraternity
to find a place for Robertson and his teammates to sleep.

The Sir Walter Raleigh Hotel in downtown Raleigh was
one of the most prominent hotels in the state, and it was so
well-known for housing statesmen and other influential citi-
zens that it was once dubbed "North Carolina's third house
of government." It also maintained a strict policy banning
black people in either the hotel or the restaurant. Just a few
years after Robertson ran up against that barrier, students
from two African-American schools, St. Augustine's College
and Shaw University, would stage protests at the Sir Walter
Raleigh Hotel that became seminal in the movement toward
civil rights in North Carolina's capital city. A group showed up
to show their opposition to the hotel's policy on July 12, 1963,
and soon police had arrested four demonstrators. Undeterred,
fifty more student protestors arrived later that day and sat on
suitcases outside the Sir Walter's entrance. The sit-in drew
five hundred spectators and embarrassed the legislators who
regularly stayed at the hotel and yet sought to win the black
vote in their districts.

Coach George Smith and his employers had not taken the
stand that Robertson had hoped for when told about Raleigh's
segregated hotels, but Smith was determined to avoid another
debacle like the one in Houston. Wherever they had to stay in
Raleigh, the whole team would be together. Michigan State
coach Forddy Anderson made the same decision, so the NCSU
planners had to find an acceptable space for two entire teams,
half of their Dixie Classic guests.

Coincidentally it was Bob Kennel, who had helped Case
make an overture to Walt Bellamy two years earlier, who

was instrumental in housing the Bearcats and the Spartans. Kennel was the president of Delta Sigma Phi, a fraternity that was formed in 1957 and whose first house was the former Colonial Pines Hotel on Tryon Road near campus. The hotel had become a fraternity house, but in preparation for the 1958 Classic the members did their best to convert it back to a hotel, and they welcomed the two teams there for the three-day tournament. The fraternity's cook would prepare breakfast and lunch for the players each day, and the fraternity members would serve the meals. "We wanted to show them some hospitality," Kennel said.

Jimmy King was a pledge in the fraternity that year, and he remembers scurrying around the house, counting beds to make sure there was enough space for all of the players and finding places for the personal items of the fraternity members who had gone home for the holidays. "I remember that they liked staying at the Delta Sig house together," King said. "They were away from everybody, and they could sleep late if they wanted to. I remember sitting around talking to Oscar Robertson."

Robertson and Johnny Green's hoops reputations preceded them, and the Reynolds faithful were excited to see them play. But if not for his coach, Green and black teammate Horace Walker would have stayed behind in Michigan. Green was a senior and the team's star, but he had never made a road trip to the Jim Crow-restricted South before. He did not know exactly what he would face in Raleigh, he said, but he was uneasy about the prospect of his teammates having to stay somewhere different because of segregation.

"We had been invited to the Dixie Classic, and he was excited," Green said of his coach, Forddy Anderson. "I went into his office, and I said to him, 'Why don't you guys go, I'll just wait until you come back, I don't want to go down there.' Because I knew what the conditions were. The freedom for the African-Americans was not the same as it was for the white players. I knew that the reason my teammates wouldn't get to stay in the hotel was because of us. Whatever restrictions we had were placed on them, and they were not accustomed. He said to me, 'Look John, we will all go, and we will all stay in the same place.'"

Tom Rand was a white Michigan State guard and a friend of Green and Walker. Years later he would fondly recall hanging out with the Cincinnati players after the games. Tournament staff brought beer and snacks out to the Delta Sigma Phi house because they knew the integrated teams would not be able to go out in Raleigh at night without incident. "There we were, Cincinnati and Michigan State, rooming together," Rand said.

The lodging arrangement was certainly atypical, but both the players and fraternity members who were around the Delta Sigma Phi house during those days observed that the NCSU staff was friendly and attentive. The warmth of that fraternity house was a contrast to the more sterile lodging offered the next integrated team to compete in the Classic. When Utah arrived the following year for the 1959 tournament, they slept in the N.C. State infirmary, said former Utes player Joe Aufderheide. The team, which included three African-American players, did eat their meals at a hotel, he said, but the deserted infirmary, which had the advantage of being within walking distance of Reynolds Coliseum, was their home away from home. Aufderheide, who had never before had to stay in a different place because of his teammates' color, also recalled seeing separate water fountains for whites and blacks for the first time on that Raleigh trip.

Aufderheide's teammate Bill Cowan had only fond memories of that infirmary stay, and did not remember any friction between the community of Raleigh and the members of his team. One of the black players, Billy McGill, a future All-American who was the tallest Utes player, did opt out of his usual pregame assignment of leading the team onto the floor,

Cowan said, and as they ran out behind a different leader the organist played the Coliseum's usual pregame song: "Dixie." "We never thought anything about it," said Cowan, who remembered laughing about the choice of song. "It just rolled off our backs. We were young; we didn't care where we slept. We actually had a lot of fun staying at that infirmary. When we got down there, we were all so excited about going to the Dixie Classic that we didn't mind where we stayed."

The 1958 visiting powerhouses might have been denied the experience of sleeping in one of Raleigh's most historic hotels, but the Bearcats and the Spartans quickly turned their focus to the real purpose of their trip South. Only the team that could enter the arena populated with so many giants and win three games could stand on the Reynolds Coliseum floor on New Year's Eve holding a championship trophy aloft. And anyone who followed college basketball knew that this was likely to be the year when an outsider would humble the North Carolinians.

On the Friday before the tournament's opening round on Monday, the *News and Observer* reported, the Big Four faithful made a run on the Reynolds box office and claimed every last seat for the Classic's final game. As advance sales reached 71,000, the tenth anniversary tournament was already sure to break attendance records. That night, the first visiting team, the Yale Bulldogs, arrived and checked into the Sir Walter Raleigh Hotel. Joe Vancisin was the head coach of that Yale squad and he and his boys felt immediately embraced by Case, Willis Casey, and the team they had assembled to welcome the 1958 field.

"The hospitality was outstanding," Vancisin said. "The hosts were tremendous. They did everything for you. They just treated us royally."

It wasn't Vancisin's first Dixie Classic experience—he was an assistant coach on the 1954 Minnesota team that came within one point of unseating N. C. State in the final—but it was Yale's first trip, and they were grateful to be there even if they were the least heralded of all of the visitors. Rounding out the visiting squads was Louisville, a 4–3 team fresh off a consolation final loss in the Bluegrass Holiday Festival, a tournament that had been won by North Carolina. Even with Yale's losing record factored in, it was the consensus that the Dixie Classic had never greeted a stronger field. Greensboro *Daily News* columnist Smith Barrier's eagerness for the spectacle that was to come in Raleigh was palpable in his December 29 offering:

"Blue-eyed Connie Pinyoun as Queen of the Dixie Classic will reign at the inaugural ceremonies at 2 o'clock this afternoon, but from that moment on, all the eyes will be red," Barrier wrote. "Red from fire, from blood, from exhaustion. It is that sort of a basketball tournament, almost greater than Everett Case's most fantastic dreams 10 years ago. Here comes the 10th annual Dixie Classic with no possible favored entry, despite the fact that the nation's No. 1 team is a participant. But ol' Ev almost outplanned himself with the 1958 field: Four teams from the nation's top 10. That's what brings out the fire and the blood, and the fans."

The most memorable Classic, the one against which all others would one day be measured, was about to begin.

Eight

On the day before the 1958 Classic opened, the *News and Observer* ran a large picture of Robertson next to a story that focused on the scarcity of tickets and the hype surrounding four top-ranked teams. If an undercurrent of racial tension accompanied the preparations for Robertson, Green, and Bryant's arrival, it received no play in the local paper. Instead, sports editor Dick Herbert speculated that either Cincinnati or Michigan State could be the team to break the Big Four's streak of winning fourteen opening Classic games in a row. With Wake Forest slated to face Cincinnati and Duke matched up with Michigan State in the first round, that record seemed to be in imminent peril.

Bill Hensley was the sports information director at N.C. State from 1954 to 1960 and in that post he generated publicity about a continuous parade of all-white athletes. As the 1958 visitors arrived in Raleigh, Hensley had the feeling he was witnessing a signal of enduring change. "Race was an issue, because none of the Big Four teams had black players," Hensley said. "You had the feeling that you were seeing a renaissance."

As he prepared to welcome his guests on the tenth staging of his signature event, Everett Case asserted, "I don't think there is any question about this being the strongest field we have ever had for the Classic." With nine years and nine trophies staying in North Carolina, Herbert even wondered in his column whether an outside champion might be necessary to preserve the strong national reputation of the tournament.

"The dominance of the Big Four is not expected to last long," Herbert said. "There will be no great shedding of tears if there is a Classic champion from outside the Big Four. The tournament does not need much to help it, but before teams around the country get the idea it is impossible to win here it might be well for a visitor to take the title."

Raleigh *Times* sports editor Bruce Phillips unfurled a flashy backdrop for the tournament with a special spread devoted to the Dixie Classic that opened, "The golden curtain on the Dixie Classic—the top offering in the apparently insatiable holiday basketball tournament mania—goes up for the tenth time in shiny William Neal Reynolds Coliseum. The grandest, gayest, gaudiest show of them all is in prospect." Phillips included the opinion of Seton Hall head coach John Russell, who had brought his team to the previous year's tournament and called the Dixie Classic "the greatest basketball tournament in the United States of America. No single cage event in the nation can match this one in competitiveness, attendance and spectacle."

It was a Monday afternoon, December 29, and fans seeking tickets were being turned away outside the Coliseum. The tenth annual Dixie Classic opened and immediately began the challenge of adding substance to the hype. Cincinnati's threat to Big Four supremacy was underscored with a first-round trouncing of Wake Forest. The Bearcats won 94–70, and Robertson scored 29 points. The undefeated Tar Heels rolled over their first-round opponent, Yale, prevailing 92–65 that day. Michigan State was also as strong as advertised, dominating Duke 82–57 to stay in the championship bracket with Cincinnati and Carolina and N.C. State, who also both won their opening games.

The Wolfpack had to endure overtime against Louisville after losing its grip on a six-point lead with just thirty-one seconds left in the game. While many of the NCSU faithful headed for the parking lot, Wolfpack players Don Gallagher and George Stepanovich each committed ill-timed fouls, the Cardinals shooters made all four free throws, and then Louisville scored for the tie after Gallagher missed his free throw in the final seconds. The Wolfpack regained its composure to prevail 67–61 in overtime, and its reward the following day would be a meeting with Oscar Robertson's Cincinnati squad.

Taking in the action that day was a three-sport high school superstar named Roman Gabriel. Gabriel was a native of Wilmington, North Carolina, 120 miles southeast of Raleigh, and he had attended basketball games at Reynolds Coliseum before. But 1958 marked his first Dixie Classic, and he had been invited there by the N. C. State athletic department on a recruiting visit. After soaking up the packed house, with four top ten teams and a raft of All-Americans, all unfolding on a stage backed by the organ and the noise meter, Gabriel needed little convincing to sign with the Wolfpack. N. C. State was close to home, and they granted him his wish to play basketball, football, and baseball.

His three-sport experiment only lasted a year. Gabriel played on all three squads as a freshman and then realized that something would have to give. He chose to drop basketball, because he showed more promise in football and baseball, and even though he remained a member of those two teams, his baseball play was eclipsed by his unparalleled accomplishments on the gridiron.

He went on to become one of the best quarterbacks in Wolfpack history. Twice he was named both an All-American and the ACC Player of the Year, and he set twenty-two school records in his time there. After college he spent fifteen seasons in the NFL with the Los Angeles Rams and the Philadelphia Eagles, where he was named to the Pro Bowl four times and named the NFL's Most Valuable Player in 1969.

Gabriel's career at N. C. State and his stellar professional

football campaign might seem to have very little to do with
Everett Case and Wolfpack basketball, but his college recruiting journey symbolized one of the controversies of Case's signature tournament. N. C. State coaches from all sports, but
especially Earle Edwards and his football staff, recognized
the Classic as a plum recruiting opportunity. In 1958, when
Gabriel was feted there, the N. C. State football team played its
home games in Riddick Stadium, which was built in 1907 with
wooden bleachers and a fieldhouse so cramped that Edwards
had his team dress for games in the Reynolds Coliseum locker
room. Through building projects with mismatched bleachers,
Riddick seated only slightly more than Reynolds. And when
Roman Gabriel, N. C. State's projected future quarterback,
came to check out the school, he never saw the stadium at all.

"I had over seventy offers," Gabriel said of his recruitment.
"I saw two games in William Neal Reynolds Coliseum, the biggest one on the planet. I never saw the football stadium, but
I was impressed with Earle Edwards. It was so impressive I
didn't care what the stadium looked like."

Three years later, when the Dixie Classic came to the end
of its twelve-year run, whispers would prevail that coaches
and administrators from North Carolina, Duke, and Wake
Forest had pushed for its abolition, because they were un-
happy about the Wolfpack's perennial home court advantage
and the recruiting edge offered by a gala event like the Dixie
Classic. With football's signing day in early February, the late-
December tournament offered a perfect campus showcase for
attractive prospects like Gabriel.

Gabriel and his fellow recruits had choice seats for the
Classic, but the first day of this most highly-touted Dixie
Classic offered very little dramatic basketball action. Only
N. C. State's overtime theatrics against Louisville hinted at the
intensity that was to come, as Wake Forest and Duke lost de-
cisively to Cincinnati and Michigan State. Wake Forest coach
Bones McKinney was happy that his squad held Robertson to

a mere 29 points, and he said after the game that he believed a team that could keep pace with Cincinnati's high-energy offense could knock off the Bearcats. "There were two things we had to do," McKinney said afterwards. "We knew we had to slow down their fast break and we knew we had to rebound. We did neither very well."

The Cincinnati-Wake Forest game in the first round is remembered today not for the score or even for Robertson's pinpoint passing, but for an altercation that occurred between Robertson and Demon Deacon big man Dave Budd. Budd was a six foot six junior with a reputation for rough play—the following season he would get into so many fights on the court that he would be suspended by the ACC. During the Dixie Classic game, he and Robertson got knotted up as they both went up to grab the same rebound. Budd gave his recollection of the tussle to the Durham *Herald-Sun* after the game:

"Robertson tripped me as we started up court a few minutes before the scuffle," Budd said. "I guess both our tempers were building up to a hot point. Then under the basket, we got tangled up in a scramble for a rebound and that was it. We fell to the floor and I was on top. I could have hit him, but I didn't. I happened to think about his race, and I knew if I hit him it would cause a lot of trouble."

Murray Greason, Jr., was the student manager for Wake Forest, and he had an excellent view of the action from the bench. For Wake Forest players and fans, it was just Dave being Dave. "Dave would say that they didn't even fight," Greason said. "They got tangled up with each other, and I think they were both aggressive and keyed up, and they were rasslin' pretty hard. But I don't think they ever threw a punch.

"Dave got a lot of press, because Oscar was the first black to play in what was basically a white basketball league in this part of the country. So some of the press picked it up and said, 'Well, it's a racial issue.' Well, that was not true. First off, Dave was not a southerner. Dave was from New Jersey. And he was an absolute equal opportunity brawler."

Robertson's account of the incident is similar. He and Budd were just two very physical players embroiled in an intense game, and Budd showed no racism, Robertson wrote in his biography, only competitive zeal. But through his entire college career, Robertson entered arenas carrying burdens that were unimaginable to any white teammate or opponent. The Dixie Classic trip was no exception. Before the trip to Raleigh, he said, he received a letter from the Grand Wizard of the Ku Klux Klan reading, "Don't ever come to the South." Then he arrived at Reynolds Coliseum for his first-round matchup against Wake Forest. Across the board, the white fans and players who were present that day remember enthusiastic fans and the Dave Budd incident, and some sportswriters even asserted that Robertson received preferential treatment from the officials because of his All-American stature. None cite specific persecution of the Cincinnati star. Robertson, remembering the tournament decades later, recalled something different.

"When I went out on the court, the arena was in a racist frenzy," he wrote in his book. "Countless times during our opening game against Wake Forest, shouts of 'nigger,' 'porter' and 'redcap' reached the court. Wake Forest's forward, Dave Budd made things worse, getting in my face and guarding me tight all night. Budd meant no malice. He was playing the game as hard as he could, the best way he could, but his antics only seemed to make the crowd crazier, and the crowd seemed to rile him up even more."

After Cincinnati defeated Wake Forest, a Bearcats fan named W. M. Wibbeler, Jr., was so upset by the reports he had heard from the Classic that he dashed off a telegram to Raleigh Mayor W. G. Enloe. The missive read, "The basketball fans of your great city have shown such ill-mannered unsportsman-like conduct and lack of appreciation for our fabulous colored basketball star Oscar Robertson that I would suggest next year confining your tournament to local teams so that you can eliminate any element of irritation to your basketball fans. The thoroughly disgusting way your fans handled themselves forms a deep impression in my mind of your city." Mayor Enloe promptly replied to Wibbeler: "Suggest you become a better informed loser. Great star Robertson and coach understand competitive sportsmanship."

At the conclusion of the 1958 Classic, Raleigh *Times* reporter Woody Upchurch wrote a column titled, "Were Negro Stars Abused?" in which he interviewed Robertson and Michigan State players Johnny Green and Horace Walker. Robertson's version of the Coliseum's climate was different than the tempest he describes in his biography. He told Upchurch, "I don't feel that the fans here were any different from any others. I don't feel that I was abused," and, later, "I have no gripe about any treatment I've received." Of course, his comments were likely to be guarded given his location and the racial climate he had observed in Reynolds.

Tom Rand, the Michigan State guard who played and socialized with Green and Walker, recalled a Dixie Classic experience that was marked by persecution of Robertson. Rand believed that some of the boos and catcalls he heard directed at "The Big O" were racially motivated, but he also noticed a striking difference between the way the Classic faithful treated Robertson and the way they treated Green. Green was friendlier and more open than Robertson, who distrusted the media and was notoriously reluctant to do interviews. Green's public impression was much more favorable that year, Rand said, and it showed.

"They actually booed Oscar every time he got on the floor," Rand said. "It was not pretty. Oscar was booed, and he was roughed up. They cheered Johnny, and they booed Oscar."

Green confirmed his teammate's account of the crowd's response to him that week. After entreating his coach to let him stay behind in Michigan, he was surprised to receive such an enthusiastic reception. It seemed to him that the fans in Raleigh had placed a bull's-eye on Robertson before he even arrived, but they regarded Green as just a talented player who put on a great show. "Let's face it: He was the number one player in the country," Green said of Robertson. "He was the villain, I guess, if you want to look at it from that sense. I was very popular, and I couldn't understand why they liked me so much, and they didn't like Oscar."

It wasn't just Green's gregariousness that endeared him to the southern fans. He came by his nickname, "Jumpin' Johnny Green," because of an extraordinary vertical leap that resulted in prodigious rebounding totals. During that 1958–59 season, when he was a senior and co-team captain, Green averaged 17.8 rebounds a game, famously pulling down 27 rebounds against Notre Dame in the Spartans' first-ever NCAA tournament appearance in 1957.

At the Dixie Classic, Wake Forest head coach Bones McKinney called Green "a kangaroo with the touch of a surgeon." His coach, Forddy Anderson, said, "There isn't a better college player in the game today." It would be hard to dispute that between Green and Robertson, the 1958 Classic featured the two most talented players in the college game, players who helped take down the tournament's color barrier with power and finesse.

In the Spartans' first Dixie Classic showdown, against a Duke team whose 2–4 record was the worst in the field, Green and company won their fifth straight game by a margin of 18 points or more, dismantling the Blue Devils 82–57. Michigan State coasted behind a stifling first-half defense that held Duke to only 14 points before halftime and the sharp shooting of Green, Lance Olson, and Bobby Andregg, a trio which combined for 45 points. Raleigh *Times* columnist Bruce Phillips wrote this about the Michigan State inside game during the tournament: "Trying to score off them inside is like facing a bear with a pair of fingernail clippers."

In dramatic fashion, Robertson and Green finished what Seth Hicks had started the year before and integrated the Dixie Classic. Everett Case, wowed with Robertson's ability, even told a reporter: "Great Scott! I know a lot of southern coaches who would like to pull a Branch Rickey with that boy," referring to the Brooklyn Dodgers owner who made Jackie Robinson the first African-American in major league baseball in 1945. But as impressive as Robertson was, it would actually be almost a decade after his Classic visit before a Big Four school would follow the lead of northern schools like Indiana and Cincinnati and recruit a black player.

Lou Pucillo, like the majority of Wolfpack players at that time, had been raised in the Northeast and was largely blind to the segregationist practices of his adopted home city. He was a senior on the 1958 team that faced Robertson and Green's squads, and after Robertson's allegations of racism came out he talked to a number of others who were there. None could remember the type of hostility that is reflected in Robertson's writings, he said, although Pucillo and others remember times when NCSU's black athletic trainer, Chester Grant, was not allowed to eat meals in restaurants with them.

To some extent, a coach's ability to end segregation on his roster was limited by his university's administration and their policies. The two state schools, N. C. State and North Carolina, admitted their first black students in the mid-fifties, meaning that if Case had successfully recruited Walt Bellamy he would not only have been the first African-American on the basketball team but one of the first on the campus at large. Meanwhile, the two private schools, Wake Forest and Duke, were not bound by the state law requiring desegregation, and trustees at the Baptist and Methodist colleges were entrenched in the all-white status quo. Finally, in 1962, eight years after the landmark *Brown v. Board of Education* Supreme Court decision made integration the law of the land, the first black student enrolled at Wake Forest. The following fall, five black students were admitted to Duke.

With the racial wall on campus newly toppled, a Virginia high school basketball star C.B. Claiborne was courted by both Duke and Wake Forest. He connected immediately with Bones McKinney, who had reportedly been eager to recruit black players for years but was constrained by university policies, but Claiborne saw more promise for himself at Duke, where coach Vic Bubas had directed his team to consecutive NCAA Final Fours in 1963 and 1964.

Claiborne became the first black athlete to play for a Big Four school in 1965, and the following year North Carolina brought in Charlie Scott, whose talent made him a household name and the first African-American college player to earn star status in North Carolina. Wake Forest and N. C. State followed suit in 1967, when Charlie Davis became a Demon Deacon and Al Heartley signed with the Wolfpack.

Claiborne, Scott, Davis, and Heartley each had moments of triumph on the basketball court and more numerous periods of isolation on campuses where almost no faces matched their own. They were pioneers, and future stars like David Thompson, Michael Jordan, Tim Duncan, and Grant Hill owed them a debt. But none of those groundbreaking players ever had the opportunity to play in the Dixie Classic, canceled four years before Claiborne broke the color barrier.

Oscar Robertson, John Bryant, Johnny Green, Horace Walker, and Seth Hicks were a different breed of pioneer, doing their small part to raise awareness in an era where blissful ignorance seemed to be the rule of the day. The Dixie Classic was a tournament named for a moniker of the Confederate South, and its programs reprinted the lyrics to the song "Dixie," which began, "I wish I was in de land ob cotton, Old times dar am not forgotten." It was an unforgettable tournament imbued with warm memories for almost everyone associated with it, but Robertson took a different view. And as he and his fellow African-Americans stood firm and nudged those early barriers down, those who came later presided over a new landscape in college basketball, where the court finally became a place where quickness, strength, and shooting chops opened the same doors for athletes of all colors.

Nine

Even as he helped his Wolfpack warm up for a first-round tilt against Louisville in the legendary 1958 annual Dixie Classic, Everett Case was able to watch enough of Oscar Robertson's domination of Wake Forest to be impressed. Since his team edged out Louisville in overtime, N. C. State was next to face Robertson's Bearcats, and Case was candid with the media about his apprehension in trying to defend the nation's scoring leader and his supporting cast. "I don't see how anybody can beat them," Case said of the top-ranked Cincinnati squad. But on December 30, with his beloved organ providing background music and a raft of his pet traditions adding spice to the event, the host team would attempt to put substance over style as they took the floor in a second-round matchup with the Bearcats.

Fans might have booed Robertson in his first appearance in Reynolds, but the local newspapers were smitten with the All-American and his unique combination of quickness and strength. The Greensboro *Daily News* devoted the top half of four sports pages to Robertson's theatrics in its report from the Classic's opening day—a spread of eight large photos capturing Robertson in action. The continuous headline narrated the action in poetic style: "Cincinnati's 'Big O' Dribbles ... Drives ... And Hooks for Score ... Rebounds ... Rebounds ... And Defends ... And Then Drives Some More."

Case had crafted this large holiday stage a decade earlier, and the tournament was exploding in every way. He told one reporter during the event that the first Dixie Classic, in 1949, had netted only $18,000, and the 1958 Classic was slated to take in between $75,000 and $100,000, to be divided among the participating teams. Case's creation was now threatening to smother his team under the hype devoted to the two top visiting teams. As observers seemed ready to concede the Classic title to Cincinnati or Michigan State, Case and his squad sharpened the fine points of their zone defense and took the floor against the Bearcats. Their plan to contain Robertson involved assigning six foot guard Dan Englehardt to cover him from the front and six eight center John Richter to cover him from the rear.

That "mixed-up zone defense," as Case affectionately called it, turned out to be Cincinnati's undoing. The Wolfpack came out early in the game determined to shut down Robertson's prolific scoring, and they discovered that he was stoppable, at least for a while. "The Big O" only managed to convert eight points in the first half, allowing N.C. State to build an 18–11 lead in the first ten minutes. Case had coached his team to slow down the speedy Cincinnati offense, which made its living off of the fast break. The technique worked, sparking State's early lead and taking the Bearcats out of their rhythm. "They made us play it their way," said Cincinnati coach George Smith. The home team never trailed again, triumphing 69–60 in a game that left a wake of emotional coaches and players and hoarse Reynolds spectators.

"Almost as if by signal, the stands rose in unison to roar a mighty ovation for the Wolfpack, an ovation which all but drowned out the final buzzer in recognition of one of the finest victories ever by a State College basketball team," wrote Moses Crutchfield in the Greensboro *Daily News*.

Robertson, who was notoriously ill at ease with the media in his collegiate career, brushed past the Raleigh *Times'* Bruce Phillips, saying, "Don't talk to me. Baby, I'm through," and made a beeline for the showers after the game. He finished with the same 29-point output he scored in the first round, but his teammates struggled to convert when faced with the immovable inside force of Richter, who grabbed 15 rebounds and scored 26 points in "his greatest effort ever for us," according to Case, who added, "Richter played those last ten minutes on guts alone." Bob MacGillivray, who pitched in with six rebounds and 16 points, said afterward that Case had set them up in his pregame talk, telling the team that a Dixie Classic win against Cincinnati would be the greatest victory the team had ever accomplished. "We were really inspired," MacGillivray said.

Cincinnati was humbled and State happily exhausted, and three-fourths of the games in the Classic's 1958 championship bracket were still ahead. When the tournament was in the books, observers were united in their belief that December 30 and 31 of that year had set the stage for two of the greatest days of Big Four basketball in history. The next contest on that docket was a 9:30 P.M. matchup between Carolina and Michigan State. Both teams had achieved easy victories on opening day, but the cakewalk was over, and Johnny Green's Spartans were confident that they could survive in the hostile territory that had already taken down their housemates.

A host of Tar Heel fans made the short trip from Chapel Hill to cheer on their undefeated team, but Michigan State showed incredible defensive tenacity, collecting 57 rebounds in the game to Carolina's 38. Even though Carolina captain Lee Shaffer hit a hot shooting streak to score 13 straight points in the second half, it wasn't enough to defuse the explosive Spartans, who prevailed 75–58. Johnny Green and Horace Walker carried the offense with a pair of double-doubles— Green with 20 points and 14 rebounds and Walker with 14 points and 12 rebounds. The victory inspired some spirited postgame revelry in the Michigan State locker room, over- heard by Greensboro *Daily News* writer Gene Warren.

"Undefeated Michigan State threw a wild, ear-shattering celebration in the dressing room after it struck down Carolina's previously unbeaten Tar Heels 75–58 here tonight to reach the finals of the Dixie Classic," he wrote. "'One ... one ... one,' the players kept shouting as they banged on the lockers and jumped up and down like kids who have suddenly been given the world. It meant one to go for the Dixie title, which has never been won by an outside team in the past nine years."

The victory was sweet redemption for the Michigan State players who still remembered the NCAA semifinals of 1957, when the Tar Heels pushed the Spartans to three overtimes to prevail 74–70 in Kansas City. Johnny Green was a sophomore on that team, and the defeat still stung, especially when North Carolina went on to defeat Kansas—again in three overtimes—for the national championship the next day. Most of the stars from the national title team had moved on by the time the 1958 Classic rolled around, but the memories were still strong for Michigan State.

This time, with the Spartans out-rebounding the Tar Heels 57–38 and a more mature, more athletic Green creating a stifling presence, the local team would have no last-second theatrics and no overtime periods. UNC coach Frank McGuire had high hopes going into the tournament—his team had won the last two Dixie Classics and, earlier in December, the Bluegrass Invitational in Kentucky. But he declared Michigan State the best team they had faced so far that season, and he even expressed reluctance to go from such an emotional loss into the consolation bracket, where the best prize was third place.

"Losers should go home," McGuire told the Raleigh *Times*. "Our boys played their hearts out. It will be hard for us to be up for them. Our boys played such a whale of a game last night and it remains to be seen whether they can come up with another good one tonight. We will do a lot of experimenting against Cincinnati."

The Michigan State players, ears ringing from their locker room spree and confident that the trophy could be theirs in twenty-four hours, were nonetheless feeling the effects of their physical outing against the Tar Heels. They did what they needed to do to win, but UNC defenders like Lee Shaffer and Dick Kepley, who fouled out in the game, had used as much force as they could muster to stop the Spartans' speedy attack, said Tom Rand, who was a guard on the MSU squad. As they retired back to the fraternity house, several Spartans were bruised, and Horace Walker, a star against North Carolina, was icing a sprained ankle. "We were pretty much in a shambles by that time," Rand said.

Not a single ticket remained as the final day of the 1958 Dixie Classic dawned. The top four teams in the field—N. C. State, Michigan State, Cincinnati, and North Carolina would square off for first through fourth place in the tournament, with the consolation final between the Tar Heels and the Bearcats slated for the 7:00 P.M. session and the Wolfpack and the Spartans prepared to usher in 1959 with a 9:00 P.M. start on New Year's Eve.

McGuire might have expressed concern about his team's ability to rally for a big-time opponent less than a day after a grueling semifinal defeat, but as the consolation final began those words seemed to be a misdirection ploy aimed at making Cincinnati overconfident. North Carolina came out with gusto, shooting 54.2 percent in the first half which sparked a 45–42 lead at halftime. But the Bearcats did not let up either, and both teams seemed to be putting on a shooting clinic for the raucous Reynolds Coliseum crowd. Cincinnati, which averaged 50.7 percent from the field for the game, pulled to a five-point lead with 3:56 remaining and seemed poised to put the Tar Heels away.

But then Carolina, led by Pennsylvanian Lee Shaffer, built its own lead, and Shaffer's basket and free throw with thirty seconds remaining made the Tar Heels' edge 90–86. Eight seconds later, Robertson plowed through a sea of blue for a driving lay-up that shrunk the lead to 90–88. UNC held the ball for a few seconds, Shaffer attempted a shot that did not fall, and Cincinnati's Mike Mendenhall recovered the ball. But he slipped and fumbled, giving the Tar Heels possession and a momentous victory that seemed to hold more in the balance than just a third-place trophy.

"It was just like winning the championship," Tar Heel sophomore star York Larese said after the win. "I don't know but that it was just a little better than winning the title. It seems that way at the moment, at any rate."

Maybe it was because the much-hyped Cincinnati Bearcats, with the top scorer in the nation leading their squad, came to Raleigh and left 1–2. Decades later, Tar Heel and Wolfpack fans engaged in a little selective memory, and many asserted that Cincinnati did not win a game at that Dixie Classic. But even though they did grab one victory on the first day against Wake Forest, the Bearcats were not able to prevail when the stakes were high. Oscar Robertson was the picture of consistency in Reynolds, scoring 29 points in each of his three outings to become the top scorer for the tournament, but he did not come close to Ernie Beck's 1952 record of 100 total points. The Bearcats' two losses in Reynolds Coliseum comprised half of their total losses that season, which ended with a record of 26–4 and a trip to the Final Four.

With the consolation final thus settled, the collective blood pressures seemed to rise in the Coliseum as tournament officials quickly reset the arena for championship. That afternoon, Captain Lou Pucillo and N. C. State's three other seniors, John Richter, Bob MacGillivray, and George Stepanovich, had a private meeting to discuss how badly they wanted to beat Michigan State for the title. Just before game time, Everett Case was in top form as a motivator, reminding his players that they could claim either a big trophy or a little one that night. With that big trophy in their sights, Case and his team waited in the Reynolds tunnel as the faithful home crowd gave a tepid reception during Michigan State's player introductions. Then the N. C. State players made their big entrance, buoyed by a packed house that hadn't seen their beloved Wolfpack take a Dixie Classic title since 1955.

Just like the other players and fans in attendance, the Wolfpack had marveled at Johnny Green's aeronautics during the first two days. They harbored no false confidence, but Case had installed a plan, leaning again on the zone defense, that would contain Green's impact and put N. C. State's senior stars on center stage. Michigan State's game plan centered on shutting down Richter, the Wolfpack big man who had been such a dominating force against Cincinnati the day before. They did slow him down; Richter had only 16 points, ten fewer than in the second round game. But as the Spartans covered the inside and Richter, NCSU senior guard Lou Pucillo poured in 22 points from outside to make up the difference.

It was one of those Wolfpack wins that unfolded better than even Case could have scripted it. The home team once raced to a 17-point lead and was out-rebounding the Spartans by 11 at the half. Most significantly, NCSU held Green to only four points and six rebounds, and Walker, with a sore ankle from the Carolina game, spent thirteen minutes on the bench and scored just 12 points. Louisville head coach Peck Hickman, watching the game after his team finished sixth in the Classic, told a reporter that no team in the nation could defeat State the way they played that New Year's Eve. "They just about played a perfect basketball game," he said. "We were inspired," said Wolfpack forward Bob MacGillivray.

Virtually everything went right for Everett Case and his team during that 1958 Dixie Classic, except for the silence he was forced into that night as his team celebrated their seventh

Classic championship. Through three of the most intense games State ever played in the tournament, the Old Gray Fox so strained his vocal cords that he couldn't talk at all after the Michigan State win and was forced to hand over postgame press conference duties to assistant coach Vic Bubas. He also had to let his smile do the talking in the postgame awards celebration, when typically he would address the Reynolds crowd from the floor.

Case's silence wasn't the only thing that looked a bit different at the Wolfpack's victory celebration. For nine years the Dixie Classic Queen had been called upon to present the trophies to the winning team members and to the most valuable player, but that night the trophy presenter was Governor Luther Hodges. Connie Pinyoun, who served as the Queen that year, said she was told that she would not assume that duty because of the concerns that could arise when she gave a trophy to one of the visiting African-American players, especially if, as many assumed, Oscar Robertson dominated and took MVP honors. The MVP was, in fact, John Richter from N. C. State, but Pinyoun stayed off the floor during the presentations nonetheless.

Laryngitis notwithstanding, Case could look back on the tenth edition of his tournament as a near-perfect specimen of what the event was meant to be. Four of the top six teams in the nation had come and played to their potential. The visiting teams charged in with gusto and threatened to unseat the Big Four if they let their guard down for even a minute. The visiting field and the local teams had so much parity that it was only the second time in Dixie Classic history that no two Big Four teams faced each other through the run of the tournament. And through some of the most grueling battles that they had ever played in their grand arena, the Wolfpack players clinched the Hollywood ending by keeping the trophy right there in Reynolds. It was the last Dixie Classic championship they would ever win.

No one doubted that N. C. State worked hard for the title, but some of the visiting coaches and players attributed another edge to the Wolfpack that year—the officiating. It was Case's tournament, and Case hired the officials, so grumbling about favoritism had long been part of the Classic landscape. Cincinnati coach George Smith turned up the volume on those complaints in 1958, especially after Cincinnati's first-round win over Wake Forest that nearly led to a brawl between Robertson and the Demon Deacons' Dave Budd. According to Robertson's memoir, he endured a variety of uncalled fouls during that contest, and Smith's vehement objections fell on deaf ears. After the game, Robertson said, Smith stormed into the officials' dressing room to unload his opinion of their performance.

In Robertson's book he also tells the story of his brother Henry, who had come to Raleigh to watch the tournament with some friends and was overheard in the locker room complaining about the abuse Robertson had taken on the Reynolds floor. "He was in another part of the locker room, remonstrating with a few members of the Cincinnati athletic department," Oscar Robertson recalled. "Any remarks about how I'd been treated on the court fell on deaf ears. My brother was bluntly told he had no business being at the game. He should have stayed home in Indianapolis."

The next day, when his team lost to Carolina, Smith confronted referee Len Toff in a Coliseum corridor after the game, according to the Raleigh *Times*, telling Toff, "You didn't give us a fair shake out there tonight." A Cincinnati official then grabbed Smith's arm to guide him away from the fray, telling the coach, "Come on, we should have had better sense than to come into this [expletive] country anyway."

Green, who went on to a fourteen-year NBA career, was so memorable in that Classic that Wake Forest coach Bones McKinney called him the best player in the tournament, waxing, "Green is as quick as a cat and as deceptive as a Russian smile. He could be the first man to go into orbit." But Green was effectively shut down in the final game and his team went home with second-place trophies. More than forty years after the event, he was in Las Vegas and he had an amusing conversation with a man who was in Reynolds that December and had never forgotten Green's feats.

"I happened to be in the lobby, and a fan came up to me and said, 'Jumpin' Johnny Green! I remember you from the Dixie Classic.' He said, 'Do you know why you came down there and couldn't beat us? It's because you played five against seven. We had the officials. Everybody knows that you can't come down there and win when it's five against seven.' Then he laughed and laughed and laughed."

When the final had concluded and the governor had handed out all the trophies it was already nearly 1959. The players and coaches from Cincinnati and Michigan State caravanned back to their fraternity house to greet the New Year, knowing that any celebration they took part in would be low-key, that they wouldn't be sampling any Raleigh nightlife on that holiday. "We tried to make the best of it, but it was New Year's Eve," Green said. "Here we couldn't go out into the city, because of the limitations and everything."

By the end of that season, Oscar Robertson would be the leading scorer in the nation for the second year in a row. His Bearcats would finish ranked number five in the nation, higher than any of the other teams in that Classic field. (N. C. State, Michigan State, and North Carolina finished sixth, seventh, and ninth respectively in the final AP poll.) His senior season and a guaranteed star turn in the NBA were still ahead, and in many ways, Robertson seemed to be living the American dream. But that New Year's Eve, in the middle of the 1950s American South, Robertson stayed up late with Green and other friends, questioning a culture where even basketball seemed to be laced with injustice.

"Even though we'd lost two out of three in the tournament, we wanted to do something to bring in the new year," he wrote. "So the black players from our team and from Michigan State's squad had an impromptu party in the fraternity house. I remember that we got some pizzas and some beer and hung out in the lounge until three or four in the morning, talking about the way the world was and why this shit happened to us."

Ten

Billy Packer was a Pennsylvanian, a high school basketball coach's son who learned to dribble and walk about the same time. But he was too far North to be touched by Dixie Classic fever, and until he came to Winston-Salem to play for Wake Forest University he had never even heard of the tournament. As a freshman, excluded from competition as all freshmen were, he watched the Classic attentively because he admired Oscar Robertson.

A quick guard who was mostly recruited by Ivy League schools, Packer had long entertained a childhood dream to play for Duke. But he was only five foot nine, and the Blue Devils showed little interest in him. Not only had he never heard of the Dixie Classic, he had also never heard of Wake Forest, until he received a recruiting visit from the man who never left anything but an indelible impression—Bones McKinney. Frustrated by Duke's rebuff and motivated by the chance to beat the Blue Devils, Packer accepted McKinney's offer to play for WFU.

The Dixie Classic had been staged for a decade at that point, and only one Big Four team had yet to take home a title—Wake Forest. As much hype had surrounded the competition at the 1958 Dixie Classic, virtually none of it swirled around the Demon Deacons, who limped through that season, finishing 10–14. Despite tenacious play from Dave Budd in the Classic, they were soundly defeated by Cincinnati in the first round and ended up beating Yale in the consolation final to finish seventh out of eight teams.

As Case and Willis Casey finalized details for the 1959 Dixie Classic, the Demon Deacons still stood a good distance from the spotlight. Most of the pre-tournament focus was going to visiting teams like Utah, who arrived in Raleigh ranked number six in the nation with an 8–0 record, and the Holy Cross Crusaders, who were also undefeated. On the day before the tournament opened, Dick Herbert of the *News and Observer* even speculated that every Big Four team might fall in the first round. Everett Case's defending Classic champions were entering the event with an uncharacteristic 2–5 record, but he declined to predict a favorite from the field he had assembled. "I wouldn't pick a winner," Case said. "I think it's pretty even."

The 1959 Dixie Classic might have lacked the flash of the previous year, but the event still cornered the market on unpredictability, as the tournament opened with the felling of three favorites—host team N. C. State, Holy Cross, and Utah. Just a year after surprising the national powerhouses and winning the title, the Wolfpack fell victim to Dayton's slowdown offense and lost 36–32. It was the first time "stall ball" made an appearance in the tournament, but it was an approach that would prove even more valuable later for the eventual champion. The State loss set Classic records for fewest combined points in a game, with Case directing his players to set such a snail's pace that the score at halftime was just 19–17 in State's favor.

The Flyers eventually prevailed, successfully accelerating the pace enough to outscore the Wolfpack. But years later, the box score of that particular game would be examined with particular interest by those who thought that certain N. C. State players were intentionally giving less than their best effort. Senior captain Don Gallagher distinguished himself with 11 rebounds, but he only managed to score five points in the game. And the Wolfpack players blew a chance at a comeback when they missed seven straight free throws in the final eleven minutes. Dayton coach Tom Blackburn later said that State controlled the offense masterfully and probably would have prevailed if not for their struggles at the free-throw line.

Undefeated and poised with confidence that an outside team would eventually prevail, Utah nonetheless stumbled right out of the gate. The Utes were up against a Duke team competing in its first Classic under a head coach who was new to the Blue Devils but as comfortable in Reynolds Coliseum as any man alive. Vic Bubas had never missed a Dixie Classic—he was an N. C. State player in the first two and a Wolfpack assistant coach under Case in the next eight. Earlier that year, Bubas had surprised the Wolfpack faithful when he accepted the top job at Duke at the age of thirty-one. He would stay in that post for ten years, leading the Blue Devils to four ACC championships and three Final Four appearances. He had propelled his new team to a 4–1 start going into the tournament, but the opening-round win against favored Utah was truly Bubas's coming-out party. Duke won 63–52 behind careful defense and double-digit scoring from five different players.

"Playing cautiously and cleverly on offense and throwing up a tight zone defense, Duke held Utah to its lowest point total of the season," the *News and Observer* recorded. "It was a return to the Coliseum for Coach Vic Bubas, who had a hand in many State victories here, and it was a splendid exhibition of all-round basketball work and planning."

Meanwhile, Wake Forest quietly started paving its own historic road with a 80–71 victory over Holy Cross that showcased the long-range shooting of Packer and the inside tenacity of senior Dave Budd. Budd, WFU's leading scorer the previous season and the player known for getting into a tussle with Oscar Robertson at the 1958 Dixie Classic, scored 17 points for the Deacs, but the real surprises of the day came from two upstart sophomores—Packer and center Len Chappell. Packer led all scorers with 25, making his biggest windfall on jump shots behind screens set by Budd or Chappell. Chappell contributed 17, 14 of them in the second half. Bones McKinney, who had been promoted to Wake Forest head coach after Murray Greason's retirement in 1958, told the press that the opening win had injected his team with vital confidence heading into a second-round tilt with Dayton.

"This is *the* game of the Dixie Classic," said McKinney, whom the *News and Observer*'s Grady Elmore described as "hoarse, perspiring and weary." "If you win this one, it means so much more. How are you going to get them up for consolation?"

North Carolina also came away with a definitive 72–65 win over Minnesota, appearing in its third Dixie Classic and becoming the only visiting team in history to play in the tournament more than twice. So, contrary to predictions, only N. C. State would enter the second day of competition in the consolation bracket. More than ever, Everett Case seemed to be falling victim to his own ambitious vision; by elevating basketball at N. C. State and prodding the other Big Four schools to keep pace, his teams were being overshadowed by the rivals that had once been easy prey.

Wake Forest's momentum snowballed in the second round with a 61–50 win over Dayton, and Carolina's York Larese hit 21 of 21 free throws and scored 37 total points to aid his Tar Heels in a 75–55 romp over Duke. For the second time in four years, Wake Forest and Carolina would face off for the Dixie Classic title, and McKinney set about instituting a game plan that could finally net them the trophy. His players did not know it yet, but McKinney was approaching the game armed with a tactic that frustrated fans and made scorekeepers the idlest workers in the arena. It was the same tactic Dayton had used against N. C. State—stall ball.

In stall ball, a coach would direct his players to grind the offense to a halt, using controlled passes and tight defense to drastically limit scoring opportunities. It had been part of the college game since the days of James Naismith, but it was later used to great effect by UCLA's John Wooden and Frank McGuire's successor Dean Smith, who popularized a slow-down scheme known as the "Four Corners" offense. In one extreme example of this approach, in 1973 Tennessee defeated Temple 11–6 in a game that prompted one writer to vent, "With no shot clock to stop them, the underdog Owls decided before the game that no matter how ugly or boring it was, or how badly they desecrated the game, they were going to stall." It was opposition to stall ball that led the NCAA to introduce the shot clock to the college game in 1985, a rule change that had been instituted in the NBA thirty years earlier.

Billy Packer was a spirited nineteen-year-old and had already taken the Classic by storm so far with games of 25 and 19 points. While he may not have grown up admiring the Dixie Classic, now that he had made the tournament's acquaintance he was ready to burn through the field to win it all. But when Packer and his teammates brought their verve and intensity into the Demon Deacons' locker room that night before the final, McKinney surprised them with the game plan: keep the ball away from the basket.

"We're in the locker room, and Bones says, 'We're not going to shoot the ball in the first half. We're going to hold the ball,'" Packer recalled. "So although I was just a sophomore, I understood basketball and coaching, and I'm thinking, 'This is ridiculous.' I was cocky. I was thinking, 'Let's play.' I was listening, but I was kind of teed off about it."

McKinney believed that the Tar Heels were deeper than his team and that the officials assumed they were going to win and would probably be quick to assess fouls on the underdog Demon Deacons. By instituting a slowdown, he hoped that he could limit the damage Carolina's physicality could cause the Demon Deacons and keep his own big men out of foul trouble.

His containment policy worked in the first half, which ended in an 18–18 tie. Then at halftime, he saw his players pawing at the gates like a bunch of thoroughbreds and decided to let them loose.

"It's brilliant what Coach did," Packer remembered. "He said, 'We can't afford any foul trouble, so I only wanted to play them a half game. We've got them right where we want them. Now let's go out the second half and play the game.' We didn't understand the strategy and what he was thinking until halftime. It was almost like a reverse pep talk."

Nothing came easy for the Deacons during the second half, but they had an answer for every Carolina basket. The teams traded leads until seven minutes were remaining, when Wake Forest gained a 44–40 edge. Wake Forest protected that lead until the final minutes, when Carolina big man Lee Shaffer and guard John Crotty made key baskets to bring the Tar Heels within one point with twelve seconds left on the clock. It was time for Packer, who had been Wake Forest's Classic hero since the tournament's opening tip, to come through. He drew a foul and then calmly made both free throws with five seconds left to clinch his Demon Deacons' first-ever Dixie Classic title.

The always-effusive McKinney was beside himself. "It is finally over!" he shouted before climbing the ladder to snip down the nets after what he pronounced his greatest victory ever as WFU's head coach. This Baptist preacher was never at a loss for words, but he still struggled to find sufficient accolades for the scrappy five nine sophomore who seemed to come out of nowhere but would one day be a household name for basketball fans. Billy Packer scored 61 points in the three games and shot with fifty-seven percent accuracy.

"When Billy Packer went to the free throw line with five seconds left on the clock, he faced the greatest test of any sophomore basketball player I have ever known," McKinney said. "And when he made both of them to give us this victory, I told myself right then that Packer could be the greatest sophomore that ever played the game."

Packer was the only sophomore to ever be named Most Valuable Player in Dixie Classic history. It was the first triumph on a big stage for the man who would become a fixture in the limelight as an iconic sportscaster whose career was defined by calling the biggest basketball games in the nation. In a thirty-six-year broadcasting career, Packer covered thirty-four Final Fours as the lead college basketball analyst, first for NBC and then for CBS. He retired in 2008 to his home in Charlotte—his tenure behind the microphone far eclipsing anything he did as an upstart Demon Deacon player. But for the Wake Forest faithful, Packer and the Dixie Classic would always be synonymous.

From a choice seat on the lower level, Murray Greason, Jr., was elated as he watched Wake Forest seal the victory. Then in his first year of WFU law school after finishing his undergraduate degree there, Greason had grown up enveloped by Demon Deacon basketball. His father became the head basketball coach before the younger Murray was even born, and had turned the reins over to McKinney just two years earlier. The senior Greason was still working for the university as the assistant athletic director, and he had given his son his seats and found a place to watch the action just behind the Demon Deacon bench.

In his twenty-three seasons at the Wake Forest helm, Greason had labored to a record of 285–239 and presided over the years in the mid-fifties when his teams began to regularly defeat North Carolina and N.C. State. In sharp contrast to the assistant who became his successor, Greason was known to be serene and controlled on the bench. "Murray Greason was different from many coaches," wrote Frank Spencer of the Winston-Salem *Journal*. "He never leaped to his feet, beat the floor or waved his arms—he just sat there burning up inside

with a keen basketball mind on fire as he directed his teams
... There he sat, never a smile or a frown crossing his face, his
chin down, his legs outstretched and his hands pushed deep
into his pants pockets."

Greason and McKinney were quite close, and in Greason's
later years he largely turned over the game preparation and
strategy roles to his excitable young assistant. That Wednesday
night, after Packer hit the final two free throws to seal Wake's
first Dixie Classic championship, Greason rushed out onto the
court to celebrate with his protégé and the Demon Deacon
players that he had helped recruit. His son remembers the celebration, and the picture that is especially vivid was one of the
shared joy between McKinney and his father. "When we won
he and Bones went out on the court and danced a jig with each
other," Greason said.

It would be an indelible image anyway, but that exultant
dance became burned in Greason, Jr.'s memory for one major
reason: it was the last time he saw his father alive. "My girlfriend, who's now my wife, and I made our way down into the
depths of the Coliseum, which I was familiar with because I
had been the manager under Bones for the past two years,"
Greason said. "I got to the Wake locker room, where I en-
countered some brainless guard who would not listen to why
I wanted to go in. So I just gave up and left. So the last time I
saw my father alive, he was dancing with Bones."

An avid hunter, the senior Greason left alone the morning after the Dixie Classic for a hunting trip in Eastern North
Carolina. On Friday morning, January 1, he was on his way
back home to Winston-Salem when his car struck the support
of a bridge on Highway 70 in Greensboro. He was dead on arrival at the hospital.

Greason's Demon Deacons were the first team in the Big
Four to find the Wolfpack's vulnerabilities when N.C. State
dominance was the order of the day, and Case was occasionally

critical of Greason in the heat of competition. But that same year, after the Demon Deacons had prevailed against his team for the 1953 Southern Conference title, Case said, "I can't think of anyone I'd rather lose to than Murray Greason." After Greason's unexpected death, Case had nothing but praise for his rival of more than a decade. "I am heartbroken," Case said. "Greason was a great man and a great competitor. The sports world has suffered a great loss, and I have lost an associate I admired very much."

McKinney, who owed his ascent in college coaching to Greason and was both his polar opposite and his perfect complement on the WFU bench, remembered something Greason said just after Wake's Dixie Classic triumph. "He told me the other night he thought we won the Dixie Classic because we knew how much he wanted us to. He was one of the most unselfish men in the world and had as many friends as any man I ever knew. I can't tell you how good he was to me. I never met a kinder hearted guy in my life."

Wake Forest basketball had likely never seen a higher and lower moment in just a few short days. As Demon Deacon fans sorted out their emotions and the Big Four prepared to swing into the heart of their 1959–60 schedules, a young college administrator named William Friday was in his fourth year as the president of the Consolidated University of North Carolina, which in those years included N. C. State, UNC, and the University of North Carolina at Greensboro. He inherited a system in which intercollegiate athletics were becoming more popular and more lucrative, but many in the academic establishment were determined to keep sports low on the campus radar. Friday appreciated athletics, but from the beginning of his tenure he made it clear that he would not give athletic directors and coaches free reign at his universities.

"When Bill Friday became acting president of UNC in 1956, the issue of intercollegiate athletics loomed so large as to threaten the stability of the UNC structure," wrote Bill Link in Friday's biography. "With little success, his predecessors had tried to control intercollegiate sports on campus."

After its unlikely Dixie Classic title, Wake Forest went on to a 21–7 campaign that ended with an ACC regular-season championship and a number nineteen postseason ranking.

The Demon Deacons weren't the only ones who had a productive year. From his New York headquarters, former Columbia and NBA player Jack Molinas was busy recruiting players who would be willing to fix their own college games to make $1,000 or more a night. Molinas had a law degree, and he was still suiting up for the semipro Eastern Basketball League, but his primary profession was making contacts on college teams from Alabama to California to Ohio. At its zenith, Molinas's network of gamblers and bookies was netting $50,000 a week with the help of players recruited at summer basketball games in the Catskills or through friends who were already involved with point shaving.

Two of Molinas's trusted associates, Joe Greene and Aaron Wagman, made some friends in Chapel Hill and Raleigh in the late fifties. Unbeknownst to Everett Case, some of those contacts were NCSU players who had already started to write their own scripts for Wolfpack games—their movements on the court not dictated by Case's defensive schemes but by the allure of a lucrative payoff.

III
SCANDAL
1960–1966

Eleven

Everett Case's infusion of Indiana tradition had gone a long way toward reshaping North Carolina's basketball landscape, but the Tar Heel State would not have become a center of the hoops universe without the influx of New Yorkers like Frank McGuire and the starting five that gave his Heels their first national championship in 1957. Even Case became fond of recruiting from the Northeast, with his rosters in the mid-fifties drawing heavily from New York, New Jersey, and Pennsylvania.

Starting in the early 1950s, New York City players who were schooled on the boroughs' blacktops began migrating out of their beloved city to play ball elsewhere. It was a rerouting that never would have taken place without the fallout from the point-shaving scandals of 1950–51, which devastated the basketball programs at former powerhouses like City College of New York and Long Island University. Lennie Rosenbluth, for one, grew up watching Long Island University and had his sights set on playing there before the program fell from grace.

But if the North Carolina schools were reaping some benefits from the New York point-shaving scandal, they were also positioned to become victim to a nefarious network, a network that wasn't eliminated by the fallout from the early fifties, but only sent into a period of dormancy. The foreboding was captured in Stanley Cohen's book about the New York scandals, *The Game They Played*: "The measure of what had occurred could not be found in numbers. One knew only that college basketball was the most corrupt team sport in America, had been for perhaps the past ten years, and indeed might yet be, for who was there certain enough to guarantee that point shaving had ended in 1951?"

Everett Case, who loved the game as purely as anyone, would soon discover that even an agricultural college with a railroad track running through the middle of it wasn't immune to the influence of big city gamblers with more than a recreational interest in basketball.

Case wasn't naïve about the threat gamblers could pose to his players, especially because most of the point-shaving exploits were being motivated and funded by Mafia kingpins in cities like New York and Chicago. He was so vigilant about steering his players away from bad influences that he brought in representatives from the FBI and the North Carolina State Bureau of Investigation to educate the players on the schemes the gamblers would employ to win the trust of athletes. In some cases, a point-fixing relationship began with something as innocent as buying a player a meal or offering to set him up with a girl. One operative in Louisiana was a barber near the Tulane campus who recruited potential fixers while he cut their hair.

"These guys came in with dark suits, and you could see the heat, and they were talking about how many millions of dollars change hands every time we play," former NCSU assistant coach Bucky Waters said of the FBI visits to the locker room. "They said, 'These people want you to change the outcome of the game, and they need you to do it. Here's what to look for.' They said, 'All they need is two players from any college basketball team in the country, and they've got a deal.'"

For men like Jack Molinas and Joe Greene who carefully put out bait to potential point fixers, there was a specific profile for the player who was most likely to bite. The best candidates typically came from poor backgrounds, and many had families to support. They were often street-smart city kids who had been exposed to gambling interests growing up. One player Molinas pursued, albeit unsuccessfully, was Connie Hawkins at the University of Iowa, who was so poor he only had one shirt, one pair of pants, and one pair of shoes, which he had to hold together with rope and wire. Molinas would play pick-up ball with Hawkins and give him a $20 bill, more money than Hawkins had ever seen. Another fixer from those years, NYU's Ray Paprocky, was married with a baby on the way and a scholarship that covered only tuition with no money for room, board, or books.

Ken Nye, who accepted a football scholarship to N. C. State in the mid-fifties, remembers trying to stretch the $15 a month he was given for spending money. Many student-athletes in those days had to find part-time jobs because they couldn't support themselves any other way. Nye, who was acquainted with some of the basketball players who were later wrapped up in point-shaving, said that they were not players who stood out in any way.

"It's a sad tale, because they were like us, they were economically challenged, and if you didn't have any money in your pocket, and a guy came up to you and said, 'I don't want you to lose tonight, but I don't want you to win by more than 15 points,' then you could rationalize that," Nye said. "So they kind of lured them in."

Smedes York was on the Wolfpack roster in those days, but he played sparingly and was never approached about point fixing ("You can't shave points from the bench," he wryly observed). Even though he was never targeted, he knew the players who were, and he doesn't believe that any tale of woe could justify what those players did to their team or their sport. A player might agree to help make the margin of victory smaller per a gambler's wishes, only to see the opposing team hit a hot streak and win by one or two points, he said. "A lot of people don't understand, there's really no difference between shaving points and throwing the game," York said. "Because at what point do you know you're going to win the game?"

Pete Brennan shared York's convictions, and he was cut from the mold that tended to get the attention of the characters in the fixing operation. He grew up in a poor family in New York City, and soon after he started suiting up for Frank McGuire's UNC team in 1955 it was clear that he was an impact player. He also enjoyed less-than-warm Southern hospitality during his first road game on the old Wake Forest campus. "I left Brooklyn and I thought it was going to be great," he said. "During my first game at Gore Gym, we won, and they were hollering, 'Damn Yankees' and throwing rocks at the bus, and I said to myself, 'God, I left New York for this?'"

But even if his adjustment was rocky at times, Brennan and his teammates helped establish their own culture in Chapel Hill, and it wasn't long before they were driven by loyalty to McGuire and to the Tar Heel program. One of five New Yorkers who started for the 1957 national champion Tar Heels, he said that none of them would have considered an overture from a gambler, no matter how strapped for cash they were. "If you need money, there's ways to make money," he said, adding that gambling was the easy way out.

He remembers that like Case, McGuire arranged a pre-season visit from an FBI agent, just in case they were not entirely convinced. "They would come in and say, 'Fellas, look, this is serious.'" Brennan said. "If you guys take even a dollar you can go to jail. And you know what? We're going to be looking. And we'll catch you taking that dollar.' So they really put great fear in you."

In the spring of 1957, still pumped from leading their team to its first national championship, Brennan and five other UNC players were trying to figure out how to get home for the summer. They found a guy who was willing to drive all six of them to New York for $5 a person, but Brennan and his roommate Joe Quigg did not have a dime. Their families did not have the means to help them, and they were out of options, so they went to see a Tar Heel booster they knew to ask him for a loan of $10, which they promised to pay back at the end of the summer. The man called McGuire, who was furious with his players and loaned them the money himself so they could get home.

"That just shows you, we didn't have anything," Brennan said. "Another thing is, we won the national championship in Kansas City, and none of our parents were there, because they were poor people. They had to listen to it on the radio."

In his efforts to keep gamblers and their wagers out of his box scores, Case did more than just host federal officers every fall. He also made every member of the Wolfpack team read a scrapbook of clippings from the 1950–51 scandals in New York. After they read the stories, each player had to sign a statement saying that he would not be involved with any gambling interest. One Wolfpack athlete who signed that pledge for four straight years was Don Gallagher.

In the summer of 1959, Gallagher reported to work as a waiter at Klein's Hillside Resort in the Catskill Mountains, where he would serve food during the day and play for the resort's basketball team at night. The Catskills were a popular summer destination of young ballplayers, providing both intense summer competition and the chance to make money at the resorts. But wherever ballplayers gathered in those years, associates of gambling kingpins like Jack Molinas were likely to be found as well, eager to get to know future college stars and recruit them to the point-shaving operation.

Another Klein's employee, Tom Scott, had become acquainted with both Gallagher and an athletic instructor named Joe Greene, and Greene asked Scott to make an introduction.

They met on the sideline of a Klein's game one summer evening, and Gallagher thought little of it. But two months later, Greene called Gallagher in Raleigh and told him that he had a way for Gallagher to make a little bit of extra money. Greene came and picked Gallagher up and asked him to consider a practice he called "arranging games." He told him that he wasn't asking Gallagher to throw a game, just to adjust the point spread to suit the gamblers' interests. Gallagher would make $1,000 a game.

"They needed to find a guy who had a character weakness and flaw, and at the time that was me," Gallagher told writer Ron Morris in 1988. "Once they get started on something like that, there are options available. But I didn't think there were any. You get in deep, then deeper and deeper."

Gallagher, who had spent a year at a military school in Virginia before college, said on his freshman basketball questionnaire that his nickname was "Taps." He was a straight-laced young man who met a girl at a freshman dance and married her less than a year later. By the time he was a senior, they already had a son. But even though he was a model student and citizen in many ways, Gallagher fit the gamblers' profile. Growing up in Binghamton, New York, he was the youngest of eight children, and his daily chore was to keep a fire burning through the night for warmth. He had the standard NCSU athletic scholarship at that time, which covered tuition, room and board, and $15 a month for "laundry expenses." During the summer of 1959, when he met Greene in the Catskills, Gallagher opted to take the job even though most of his teammates were staying in Raleigh to work out and attend summer school, because he and his young family needed the extra money.

During their meeting in Raleigh that day, Gallagher expressed interest in Greene's proposition. It was not long before Greene had assigned him his first game—between North

Carolina State and Wake Forest on December 5, 1959. It was one of eight games that Molinas and his people were involved in fixing in the first week of the 1959–60 season alone. The Wolfpack was the underdog, with the Demon Deacons favored to win by 12 points, and Greene asked Gallagher to make sure his team lost by more than the spread. Wake Forest won the game 73–59 and Gallagher collected his money from Greene. But even though he had plenty of needs, Gallagher was too nervous to spend any of the $1,000. He hid the money in his apartment, and soon he asked Greene to pay him in $20 bills so that if he did spend any of the money it would not arouse suspicion.

"When Gallagher accepted his first payoff from Greene, he was also told exactly how to fix a game," Morris wrote in *ACC Basketball: An Illustrated History*.

> Most of Gallagher's work was done on defense, where it was more difficult for a coach to detect wrongdoing. Instead of playing tight against an opponent, Gallagher occasionally sloughed off and gave up open shots. On rebounds, Gallagher often failed to box his opponent out and allowed other uncontested baskets.
>
> There were more obvious ways, but they were saved only for drastic situations. Gallagher could miss a shot intentionally, or make an errant pass, or step out of bounds on purpose. Eventually, he perfected the art of shooting at the back of the rim on free throws to intentionally miss.

The Wolfpack's next game was on the road against South Carolina, and upon arrival in Columbia Gallagher met Greene outside the team hotel to collect the money that was due him from the Wake Forest game. He also gave Gallagher some instructions about N. C. State's upcoming game against the Gamecocks: Play your very best, and there might be some extra money in it for you.

Gallagher wasn't quite sure what Greene meant, but he followed Greene's advice and played his hardest. It was later revealed that gamblers had paid South Carolina players Larry Dial and Robert Frantz $500 each to make sure that South Carolina lost by more than three points that night. The plan was thwarted when another Gamecock player, Ronnie Johnson, hit a last-second shot to give his team a 71–70 victory. The gamblers lost their bets, and neither Gallagher nor the South Carolina players collected a dime.

From that point on Greene became a frequent presence in Gallagher's life, even calling the player's Raleigh apartment and leaving cryptic messages with Betty Gallagher, who was unaware of her young husband's arrangement. Gallagher was a senior captain, with a new lucrative supply of income, but his coach could only see that the team was an uncharacteristic 2–5 going into the 1959 Dixie Classic. Everett Case was hopeful that the Classic would be a shot in the arm for his struggling Wolfpack. As Case greeted the visiting teams and drew up plans to contain Dayton in the first round, Gallagher was again meeting with Greene. This time, he would collect his $1,000 if N. C. State either defeated Dayton by fewer than four points or lost the game.

Case instructed his players to slow down the action against Dayton, and that style of offense made it very difficult for Gallagher to undermine his team's efforts. It turned out that the Wolfpack helped him out that day, combining to miss seven straight free throws in the second half. Gallagher said later that he did not do anything intentional that led to Dayton's 36–32 victory. But nonetheless, after the game he slipped into a men's restroom at Reynolds Coliseum, where Greene was waiting. Without a word, Greene slipped him a comic book. Inside was $1,000 in cash.

With N. C. State mired at 3–8 in early January, Gallagher agreed to fix the two remaining Duke-N. C. State games for the now-standard $1,000 each, to be paid in advance. In the first game, on January 9, Gallagher was supposed to help his Wolfpack lose by more than the spread of 14 points. The Blue Devils were only ahead by one with 4:27 remaining, but Gallagher starred in a comedy of errors in those final minutes to make the score 47–34. It wasn't enough, and after the game Gallagher met Greene at a Durham railway station and returned the $1,000. That dark meeting, he told Ron Morris, was the first time he truly feared for his life.

The next Duke-State contest, on February 9, 1960, came on the heels of a three-game Wolfpack winning streak. Gallagher was at the top of his game during that period, playing to divert any suspicion that his earlier missteps might have raised. He did not make any deals in those games, and he scored 15 points against Eastern Kentucky, 25 against Clemson, and 19 against Virginia. But the money beckoned, and Gallagher had agreed to fix both of the Duke games. Greene made his expectations clear for that night: The Wolfpack had to lose by at least 12 points.

For the bettors, this second game was even more frustrating than the first. With their money on Duke, the gamblers watched as N.C. State hit shot after shot, with senior Don Gallagher contributing ten points, and win the game 63–53. Gallagher feigned excitement as he celebrated the victory with his teammates, but he knew he had some explaining to do. At midnight that night, he answered a knock at his door and found a very nervous Joe Greene.

He apologized to Greene for failing to arrange a loss, but the meeting wasn't over. Greene told him that there were some people outside in the car who wanted to have a talk with him, and Greene warned Gallagher that one of the men had a gun. When they reached the 1960 Buick sedan, a man named Dave Goldberg got out and invited Gallagher to go on a walk. Goldberg was a backer for the nationwide point-shaving operation, a St. Louis-based bookmaker who met with Jack Molinas in 1957 and promised to help fund Molinas if he would find players willing to shave points. He was one of the biggest fish in the whole operation, and he was outside of Gallagher's Clark Avenue apartment in Raleigh, demanding an explanation.

Gallagher apologized profusely, explaining that he tried to pull back on a couple of lay-ups and they went in anyway. N. C. State was hot that night, and Duke was off its game, he said. Goldberg asked him to return his fee—fifty $20 bills—and they discussed what could be done to avoid similar outcomes in future games. Gallagher suggested recruiting N. C. State's other starting forward, junior Stan Niewierowski, since two players could have more of an impact than one. Goldberg agreed and returned to his car. Gallagher never saw the gun, but he was convinced Goldberg had it under his coat. During the game that evening, according to later court testimony, Goldberg had told another operative, Aaron Wagman, "Something's not right here. He isn't trying to dump the game. Somebody might get hurt here."

State was next scheduled to play on February 13 against Maryland. Still reeling from his late night encounter, Gallagher found a quiet place to talk to Niewierowski the day before the game. A New York native like Gallagher, Niewierowski was a natural athlete who was recruited by major league baseball scouts out of high school. He was also known as a guy who loved a good time, and former teammate Bob DeStefano once said of him, "Throw a feather in the air and he'd bet whether it would hit the floor or not." To Gallagher's relief, Niewierowski offered to help fix the Maryland game, and Greene promised them $1,000 each.

With Niewierowski working with him, Gallagher collected his first payoff since the Dixie Classic. The Wolfpack players were charged with making sure their team did not win by more than three points. N. C. State came in just under the wire, defeating Maryland 48–46. In 1960 the average annual income was just over $5,000, and a new car could be purchased for $2,200, so for a college kid to take home $1,000 for a night of basketball was outrageous. Greene and his cohorts were helping to make them rich, and with every game the players were deeper embroiled in an illegal operation that stretched from coast to coast. But that February, the gamblers learned that there was one game that was worth more to Gallagher and Niewierowski than $1,000.

By then the North Carolina-N. C. State rivalry had become the most feverish in the Big Four, and the Tar Heels were coming to Reynolds Coliseum on February 17. When Greene took the two Wolfpack players for a ride on the day before the game, they refused to cooperate, citing their desire to beat their favored rivals. Greene tried to negotiate, offering each of them $1,250, but they wouldn't bite. North Carolina won by four points, and Don Gallagher finished his senior season—$3,000 richer than he had started it—in early March with a loss to Wake Forest in the ACC Tournament.

That spring Gallagher, who also ran track for N. C. State, was awarded the Alumni Trophy, given annually to the university's most outstanding athlete. He graduated with honors and was recognized for being in the best platoon in N. C. State's ROTC program. "He was the kind of guy that everybody respected," said Bucky Waters, who played with Gallagher at State. "He and [former North Carolina Governor Jim] Hunt were in school at the same time. Those were two guys you would say, 'If one was to be governor some day, it would be Gallagher.'"

Case was yet unaware that his players were involved with unsavory gambling operations, but it had been a disappointing season under any circumstances. The Wolfpack finished 11–15, giving Case his first losing season in fourteen years of leading the program. They were ranked sixth out of seven teams in the ACC. But he had some talented players returning, like Niewierowski, who was named captain for the 1960–61 season. The slate would be wiped clean come November, another Dixie Classic was brewing, and Case was still in his dream job. Better things, he trusted, were ahead.

Twelve

By this point in the operation, at least a half-dozen different New York gambling operatives were arranging games in North Carolina and N. C. State was not the only school infiltrated—a UNC reserve named Lou Brown had been recruited to help get his teammates involved in the action.

Don Gallagher graduated from N. C. State with multiple honors and enlisted as an officer in the U. S. Army. Gallagher's point-shaving days were behind him, but Stan Niewierowski was still collaborating with Joe Greene and his associates, and they kept him in mind as they looked for ways to make the 1960–61 season more profitable than the previous one.

Niewierowski was the team captain, and as the season approached he had recruited two juniors into the inner circle—Anton Muehlbauer and Terry Litchfield. Les Robinson was a freshman in the 1960–61 season and as such competed only on the freshman team, but he became friendly with Niewierowski and some of the other upperclassmen. Robinson was hanging out in the dorm one day during the semester break when Niewierowski came by and asked him to go to a movie. Robinson was bored, and he was honored by the invitation from the senior team captain, so he hopped in the car.

They stopped at a bar called The Profile and Niewierowski got out, telling Robinson, "Wait there. I'll be right back." Robinson said that he wanted to go in, but Niewierowski repeated sharply, "Wait there. I'll be right back." Later, it was suspected that the man who ran the restaurant, Red Campbell, was connected with the gambling network and had at least six phone lines installed to call in bets. Campbell knew which players throughout the country were participating in fixes on any given night, and that evening Niewierowski was stopping by to put $100 down on the team that was playing Iowa, because he had learned through Campbell that some Hawkeyes players were on the take.

"I thought he was just going in there to get a beer before we went to the movie," Robinson said. "He told me, 'Stay here,' and he was doing me a favor. He did not want me to see him doing it."

Robinson was also friendly with Muehlbauer, known to his teammates as "Dutch," and he vividly recalled times when none of the guys had enough money for a pizza, and Dutch would open a case and produce a $100 bill. A naive freshman from West Virginia, Robinson thought that the junior star might somehow be making money for playing well, but it never occurred to him that Muehlbauer would get rich from playing poorly. "These guys had been coming down here giving them money and everything, they just thought they were like rich uncles, that they loved basketball, buying them clothes and everything," Robinson said. "I used to think Dutch Muehlbauer had money all the time."

Even though Niewierowski had accepted payments earlier than his younger teammates, he wasn't involved when an associate of Greene's named Bobby Kraw approached Muehlbauer and Litchfield to fix a game against Georgia Tech on November 17, 1960. Wake Forest's Billy Packer once said that Muehlbauer, a New York City product known for his tenacity on defense, was the toughest man ever to guard him. So when Muehlbauer's coach Everett Case saw a sloppy defensive effort against Georgia Tech that evening, he had an uneasy feeling. That game marked the beginning of Case's decline physically and emotionally. He would always be revered on the N. C. State campus, and he would coach for four more years and lead the Wolfpack to more memorable victories. But that Georgia Tech game, played just five weeks before the twelfth Dixie Classic was set to open, was the moment when the luster of the game was, for Case, forever tarnished. He once called it the saddest day of his coaching career.

"Things began to happen," he testified later in a Wake County courtroom. "Mistakes, poor ball handling. I began to think we were getting bad calls from the officials. It was the first game I sensed anything wrong."

Charlie Bryant was an assistant coach at Wake Forest at the time, and he was there to scout the Wolfpack and the Yellow Jackets. He did not talk to Case about it, but he came away with the same suspicions. "I went back and told Bones McKinney, 'I don't know what a fix looks like, but if there is such a thing as a fix I saw it last night.' Muehlbauer missed two or three easy lay-ups that I knew damn well he could make. Every time he got the ball he'd turn it over or do something stupid."

Even though both Muehlbauer and Litchfield accepted payments before the game, they testified later that they returned the money because they did not keep the points within the spread requested by the gamblers. And unbeknownst to them, their questionable play had put Case and others on the alert.

Pat Terrill, whose husband Lee was one of the NCSU assistant coaches, recalled a game from around that time when Lee became alarmed by some missteps on the court. In particular, Pat Terrill said, Lee told her that he had spent a lot of time on a certain inbounds play in practice, and the Wolfpack players had it down cold. But when game time came, they couldn't execute the play. Pat was frustrated by what Lee had told her and what she saw herself during one game, and afterwards she went straight down to the hallway outside the locker room. "I confronted two of the guys," she said. "I said, 'Are you guys dumping these games?' And they just looked at me, dumbfounded. On a lark, I asked the question, and it turned out later that they had."

One of the many things that was eating at Case after the questionable Georgia Tech game was the fact that he had not yet invited local lawmen to N. C. State for their annual talk to the players about point-shaving. The game was on a Saturday, and on Sunday he called NCSU athletics director Roy Clogston and asked him to schedule a session. SBI agent John Boyd came to campus the next day. "He told them what would happen to anyone caught, and he told them not to get involved because they would get caught," Case said later.

The specter of players who might be cheating loomed large for Case during those weeks, and in addition to bringing in the law enforcement officers he talked to Wake County district solicitor Lester Chalmers that fall about his fears so that Chalmers could look into it further. But Case still had a tournament to put on. Despite the turbulence, the 1960 Classic would attract the most fans ever and bring the same on-court intensity and off-court revelry that had made Raleigh the post-holiday destination for any serious southern basketball fan.

On the night before the tournament opened, the Raleigh Merchants Bureau decked out three blocks of downtown Raleigh with red, white, and blue banners, according to the *News and Observer*. The banners, which were emblazoned with pictures of basketball players to keep them from being confused with Christmas decorations, were a symbol of the business boon that the Dixie Classic continued to bring to local establishments. "Every business from the State's local liquor stores to peanut roasters will ring up added coin," the newspaper said.

One *News and Observer* reporter, Charles Craven, even devoted his December 29 article to descriptions of Classic details from the ladies' hats to the opinion of popcorn vendor Mrs.

Janice Murray. He noted a disgruntled police officer questioning the sanity of the Coliseum throng, Bones McKinney's com-
plaint that he had too many "friends" asking favors from him
when he needed to focus on coaching, and two state highway
patrolmen who had to move their cars at the behest of the
local police.

"Minutes before game time at 2 P.M. the front of Reynolds
Coliseum resembled opening day at Hialeah—rosy sky fleeced
with clouds, shoulder-warming sun and gay crowds," Craven
wrote. "Plaid garments were in profusion, lending to the sporty
atmosphere. Tyrolean headpieces dotted the mob, some with
small but brilliant plumage."

If one could somehow manage to turn away from the feath-
ered hats, there was still basketball to be watched, and the 1960
Classic field featured Maryland, Villanova, Marquette, and
Wyoming. It was the second visit for Wyoming and Villanova,
the first for the other two schools, and Villanova was the most
threatening outside team, coming in with a 4–2 record and a
high-scoring All-America candidate named Hubie White. True
to form, three of the Big Four teams were nationally ranked
entering the Classic—an undefeated Duke club at number six,
N. C. State at number ten, and Carolina at number eleven.

On paper, it seemed that Everett Case and his Wolfpack
had successfully buried the past and were determined to re-
claim the winning ways that had so long defined them. They
were 6–1 when the Dixie Classic commenced, with their only
loss coming by one point to Wake Forest on November 14.
They had even won the Georgia Tech game that caused Case
so much consternation. N. C. State, it seemed, was gunning
for its eighth Dixie Classic title, and the Raleigh paper ran
an opening-day photo of Case and several of his top players
reaching out to touch the trophy.

There is no record of Joe Greene and company's involvement in the 1960 Dixie Classic. But even without any payoffs,

the Wolfpack stumbled in the first round of the tournament
that year, blowing a 14-point halftime lead to fall to Villanova
72–63. Niewierowski had a big game on the boards with 19 rebounds, but he fouled out with five minutes left in the game.
With his ouster, said the *News and Observer*, "any chance had
of holding off the resurgent Wildcats vanished."

If tournament basketball was usually a feast for Case, that
day the pickins' at the buffet were slim indeed. The first-round
loss was bad enough, and blowing a big lead is every coach's
nightmare. To add insult to injury, when Case was talking with
a Maryland trainer later in the aisle of the Coliseum, a *News
and Observer* reporter overheard a police officer give Case a
"mild bum's rush." According to the newspaper item, "the cop
walked up and officiously growled: 'You can't stand there and
block the aisle, mister.'"

Wake Forest lost to Marquette, also in the first round, while
Carolina and Duke survived their opening games to move into
the semifinals. Duke, the highest-ranked squad coming in,
seemed like the team to beat now, especially after dismantling
Wyoming 86–59 to open the tournament.

But Carolina, paced by the strong play of York Larese with
24 points, also looked like it could do no wrong in Reynolds
that day. Frank McGuire expressed surprise at the way his
team had handled a strong Terrapins squad, crediting a varied
defense that alternated between man-to-man and three different zones throughout the game. "If you've got a good defensive club, you'll never look bad," McGuire said. "Today was
our best defensive game of the season." Carolina would face
Villanova and Duke would take on Marquette in the second
round.

After their initial stumble in that final Classic, the Wolfpack
rallied to defeat Maryland in the second round and Wake
Forest in the consolation final to finish in fifth place. In sum-
marizing the 99–91 victory over the Demon Deacons, *News and*

Observer sportswriter Joe Tiede wrote, "Those old rivals, State and Wake Forest, went at each other as if the national championship was at stake." Case told reporters after the game, "I believe this was one of the most exciting games in the history of the tournament." He also made a point of praising the efforts of Niewierowski, who scored 24 points that afternoon. "He's one of the best captains I've ever had, for leadership and things like that," Case said.

That spirited game gave birth to a tradition that illustrated both the WFU-NCSU rivalry and Coach Bones McKinney's offbeat sense of humor. At one particularly intense moment during the contest, McKinney picked up one of the chairs that comprised the team bench, held it aloft and smashed it to the ground. When Case told the story to a gathering later, he claimed that McKinney broke the chair into forty pieces.

Shortly after the tournament, N. C. State athletic director Roy Clogston wrote a letter to McKinney asking him to reimburse the hosts for the cost of the chair, which he placed at $14.33. But McKinney had a different plan. He repaired the chair, painted it gold and black on the top and red and white on the bottom, and made it a moveable trophy for the two rivals to claim any time one felled the other. For the next five years, until Case retired, the chair made regular trips between Raleigh and Winston-Salem.

The Wake Forest squad, defending champions of the Dixie Classic, was just months away from making ACC history. But the 1960–61 season opened at a crawl for the Demon Deacons, Billy Packer said, because they were hobbled by early injuries to Bob Woolard, Al Koehler, and star big man Len Chappell. They had to raid the Demon Deacons football team and lure Bill Hull and Norman Snead to the hardwood to have enough players on the roster when the season opened, and even though Chappell played in the Classic it was his first week back in action.

"By the time we get to early December, we were struggling," Packer recalled. "I think only me, Alley Hart, and Jerry Steele were left from the previous team. We eventually won the ACC Championship. But that's not who we were in December."

Day Two of the 1960 Classic opened with the Tar Heels dominating Villanova 87–67 after leading 51–26 at halftime. Wyoming coach Bill Strannigan, who was watching the game, called the first half the best twenty minutes of basketball he had ever witnessed. One reserve whose play McGuire praised after the Villanova win was a five foot nine guard named Larry Brown, who would go on to a storied coaching career in college and the NBA. Meanwhile, the Blue Devils, growing ever stronger under Vic Bubas, led nearly the whole game against Marquette to prevail 86–73. Sophomore Art Heyman, who would become a three-time All-American and the National Player of the Year in 1963, scored 29 points to lead the Blue Devils in what Bubas called "our biggest test."

The championship game of what would be the final Dixie Classic served as a foreshadowing of the rivalry that would someday eclipse all others among the Big Four: North Carolina versus Duke. In future decades no fewer than three books would be written about this rivalry alone, including one by UNC fan Will Blythe entitled, *To Hate Like This is to be Happy Forever.* More than one scribe has called it the greatest modern-day rivalry in college basketball. That night in Reynolds Coliseum, the undefeated Blue Devils would face a Tar Heels team that had looked unstoppable in the first two rounds.

Frank McGuire's greatest concern was shutting down Heyman, who averaged 25 points a game that season as a sophomore. Heyman had actually almost worn Carolina blue; he announced his intention to play for McGuire in the spring of 1959, but during his official recruiting visit later that year his stepfather and the Carolina coach got into a shouting match and Heyman had to separate the two. The agreement between the player and the school dissolved, and Bubas made him his first major recruit when he took over the Duke program.

To contain Heyman's offensive output, McGuire tapped Doug Moe, a six foot six senior from Brooklyn who had played against Heyman in their younger days on the playgrounds of New York City. Early in that final game, according to the book *Four Corners* by Joe Menzer, McGuire called a time-out, pointed at Heyman and told Moe one thing: Don't let him touch the ball again. Moe took his coach's admonition seriously. Heyman scored eight points before that time-out and only three for the remainder of the game, with Moe smothering him every step.

"Heyman was in shock," Menzer wrote in *Four Corners*. "No one held him to 11 points. No one." Moe's stifling defense wasn't the only part of his game that boosted Carolina that night. He also scored 16 points and grabbed 17 rebounds to become MVP of the Classic. He was credited with leading the Tar Heels to their 76–71 victory and their third Dixie Classic championship.

Duke had posed the sole legitimate threat to the Tar Heels at that tournament, and years later Moe, even though he brought home the MVP trophy, could remember only that his team had doled out some lopsided defeats. The 1958 tournament, featuring Oscar Robertson, stood out more for him, he said. The basketball in 1960 was below the usual standard and the host team was limping, but the Dixie Classic still shined, and as the action unfolded the local paper was able to report that Tulane, Navy, Stanford, and Illinois had accepted invitations for the 1961 Classic.

As it turned out, the players on those teams would have an unexpected holiday break. When the 1960 tournament Queen, Duke junior Delia Chamberlin, awarded the Tar Heels their trophy late that night as the crowd prepared to greet 1961, no one in the cheering throng guessed that it would be the last Dixie Classic trophy ever given, or that in just a few months the tournament's MVP would be forced to leave UNC under a cloud of suspicion and finish his college education elsewhere. No one suspected that the shadow which passed over Case's Wolfpack kingdom in that November Georgia Tech game would grow into a vast dark cloud that would soon snuff out the Dixie Classic.

Thirteen

After the 1960 Classic, N.C. State beat Virginia handily and then traveled down the road to Durham to face Duke, a team that was building a new dynasty under Vic Bubas. Before the game, according to later court testimony, Joe Greene and his associates promised Niewierowski $2,000 and Muehlbauer $1,250 to fix the game against the Blue Devils. N.C. State was leading by one at halftime, but they blew that edge and lost to Duke 81–67, commencing a four-game losing streak for the Wolfpack. A few days after the game, Niewierowski received a comic book in the mail. Tucked inside was their $3,250 in cash. It was the largest total payoff ever given to any N.C. State players.

That particular game marked a shift for the Wolfpack players who were in league with gamblers. Whereas their previous agreements had involved keeping their lead within a certain range to cover the spread, the Duke game was a straight "throwing" of a game, or making sure their own team lost so that their employers would come out ahead. As players sunk deeper into the gambling network, they often crossed the line between a fix and a throw. Jack Molinas confirmed the plan years later in an interview with New York *Post* reporter Milton Gross: "Stan Niewierowski and Anton Muehlbauer were contracted to sink North Carolina State against Duke. Joe Greene was handling the payoffs for this one, and since he was an avid fan of Batman and Captain Marvel, he mailed the money for Niewierowski and Muehlbauer inside comic books."

The Wolfpack emerged from its slump in late January, winning seven out of the last nine games before falling to South Carolina in the opening round of the ACC Tournament on March 2, 1960. March, always the favorite month of college basketball fans, opened with the exciting championship for the conference that was fast becoming one of the most competitive in the nation. But before the month was over, no Big Four fan would be able to look at his beloved sport quite the same way.

Wake Forest coach Bones McKinney had claimed Dixie Classic bragging rights in 1959, but eight years after the ACC's formation his team had yet to win a conference tournament. The 1961 event, played at Reynolds Coliseum, seemed to offer the Demon Deacons their best shot yet, especially because one of their fiercest competitors had been asked to stay home.

Increasingly vigilant in its role as the watchdog of college athletics, the NCAA had been investigating the University of North Carolina's recruiting practices in the second half of 1960, and on January 10, 1961, UNC was placed on probation for one year. The NCAA Council's report alleged that UNC coaches had paid university funds to entertain recruits and their families away from campus. Specifically, Frank McGuire and his colleagues were charged with paying for the lodging and food of prospective players' parents when they came to Raleigh for the Dixie Classic.

Probation meant no ACC tournament for the Tar Heels, even though they had finished at the top of the conference during the regular season with an ACC record of 12–2. The disqualification gave WFU the top seed and a bye in the first round. The Demon Deacons proceeded to dominate first Maryland, and then Duke in a rematch of the 1960 final, but this time Wake Forest prevailed for its first ACC title. The win would send McKinney's squad to the NCAA Eastern Regional, with the initial game against St. John's in Madison Square Garden.

The Wolfpack entered the postseason in the middle of the ACC pack with a 16–8 record, but the ball bounced on for Everett Case and his team despite the uneasy feeling he still had when he remembered that November game against Georgia Tech. He had reported his concerns and investigations into point-shaving were beginning behind the scenes, but as March of 1961 dawned the typical Wolfpack fan knew nothing of the turmoil that would soon erupt. The *News and Observer* even printed a picture of Stan Niewierowski, Anton Muehlbauer, and teammate John Punger above the caption: "On these three rest much of State's hopes for a sweep of the ACC tournament."

Those hopes, and Niewierowski's college career, ended in the first round of the ACC Tournament with a loss to South Carolina, and Wake Forest alone would carry the Big Four torch into the NCAA playoffs. Spurred on by the prolific scoring of All-American Len Chappell, the Demon Deacons took St. John's by storm in New York, winning 97–74 to send WFU to the second round in Charlotte.

It wasn't easy to beat St. John's in the Redmen's home arena, and Billy Packer and his fellow Deacons were exultant that night in New York. But by midnight or so, Packer and his teammate Alley Hart, had fallen into their beds at the team's Manhattan hotel. They were both out when Packer was awakened by a persistent knock on their door after midnight. Groggy, he opened the door and saw Dick Markowitz, an old childhood friend from Allentown, Pennsylvania, and a player for George Washington University.

GWU had lost its first-round game, but Markowitz went out with some friends in New York City and missed the team bus. It was obvious to Packer that he had been out having a good time in the city. Markowitz was six feet five inches, with dark hair and features, and he was a dapper dresser who always wore a hat. The bus was long gone back to Washington, he told Packer, he needed a place to sleep, and he thought his old friend might be able to help. One Wake Forest player, Jack Jensen, was a walk-on and the thirteenth player on the squad, so he was rooming by himself in the hotel. Packer sent Markowitz down the hall to Jensen's room, eased the door shut so as not to disturb Hart, and went back to sleep, forgetting the whole episode.

The next day, March 15, the Wake Forest squad packed up for Charlotte, where they would soon face St. Bonaventure in the Charlotte Coliseum. On March 16, according to his biography, *The Wizard of Odds*, Jack Molinas flew from his home base in New York to Washington, D. C., to make a speech at the Touchdown Club. Known for his accomplishments on the court at Columbia University, with the Fort Wayne Pistons, and in the Eastern Basketball League, Molinas was also a practicing lawyer and the secret mastermind of the nationwide point-shaving network.

Molinas was aware that Manhattan District Attorney Frank Hogan—the same man who was instrumental in breaking open the college basketball scandals in New York City ten years earlier—was suspicious of him and his associates, and he recognized one of Hogan's detectives on the flight to Washington and in the audience at the dinner. Molinas's topic that evening? "The Integrity of College Basketball." "My main point was that just because there are a couple of bad apples in the barrel doesn't mean that every apple is bad," Molinas later told New York *Post* write Milton Gross. "In spite of all the scandals and rumors of scandals, college basketball was basically an honest game."

On March 17, Wake Forest notched another NCAA victory, felling St. Bonaventure 78–73 in front of a partisan crowd in Charlotte. But they had to share the top of the sports page with a different type of breaking news: Frank Hogan's office in New York announced the arrest of two men, "described as representatives of a nationwide syndicate, and charged them with bribery and conspiracy in an attempt to rig college games." The two men were identified as Aaron Wagman, who along with Joe Greene had been involved with Wolfpack players Don Gallagher and Stan Niewierowski in early 1960, and Joe Hacken, a known New York gambler who was one of Jack Molinas's closest friends and associates.

Those first indictments out of New York involved two games with no connections to the Big Four: Seton Hall vs. Dayton on February 9 and Connecticut vs. Colgate on March 1. From that point in mid-March, every day's news seemed to bring a new and more disheartening tidbit. (Wake Forest finally stumbled in their playoff attempts, losing to St. Joseph's 96–86 in the East Region Final.)

On March 22, a new issue of *Sports Illustrated* hit the streets with an article called "The Facts About the Fixes." The article cited those close to the New York investigation, who said that many more players would be exposed in the coming weeks, including, "a number of Southern state universities." Also that day, University of North Carolina Chancellor William Aycock confirmed to the Associated Press that two New York City detectives had visited the UNC campus in conjunction with the probe. Reaction to those revelations included a column by Dixie Classic co-founder and *News and Observer* sports editor Dick Herbert, in which he urged the legal system to levy the harshest punishment possible against the guilty parties to curb any future crooked practices in college basketball.

"The penalty should be so rough that it would make the sharpies hesitate before attempting a fix," Herbert wrote. "A slight sentence for the guilty will serve only as a license fee to steal and corrupt. Laws should be strengthened to deal with these people as harshly as possible. Meanwhile, basketball coaches should continue to do all in their power to combat the evil that always will be present."

Les Robinson, the NCSU freshman guard who had been told to wait in the car while Niewierowski placed a bet earlier that year, was heading home to West Virginia for spring break on the day after that issue of *Sports Illustrated* came out. He was carpooling with Terry Litchfield, who was from Kentucky, and while they drove the two discussed the intricacies of point-shaving. The son of a coach, Robinson had heard a good bit about the New York scandals growing up, so he thought he understood how a fix was arranged, little knowing that he was sitting next to someone who had actually mastered the act.

Despite Chancellor Aycock's disclosure of the detectives' visit to UNC, none of the Big Four coaches publicly professed to know anything about local connections to the scandals at that point, and at the end of March they all went to Kansas City for the annual meeting of the National Association of Basketball Coaches. While together the coaches issued a statement taking partial responsibility for the point-shaving activity and pledging greater vigilance in the future. On April 4, a New York grand jury convened and started interviewing witnesses, with one source inside the police department predicting that the network could involve twenty or more colleges.

Allegations continued to leak out, but they were still generic to fans in the Tar Heel State. A sense of dread seemed to hang in the air that spring, but no one in the Big Four could name it. Anyone's favorite team could be guilty, or anyone's favorite team could be clean. That was the way things stood until April 28, 1961, when two Tar Heels were named and suddenly Big Four fans went from observers to victims. According to Wagman's grand jury testimony, UNC player Lou Brown had agreed to participate in the point-shaving network late in 1960. One of the first things Brown did in that role was to arrange a meeting between Wagman and his friend Doug Moe.

Brown, who was from Jersey City, never played enough minutes to be a point-shaving target himself. But he knew

plenty of fellow players, and he soon became valuable to the
New York operatives as a recruiter on Frank McGuire's team.
Moe, the MVP of the 1960 Dixie Classic, was a star for the
Tar Heels, and he was Brown's closest friend on the team. It
seemed like a natural thing for Brown to arrange a meeting
and ask for Moe's collaboration on the scheme. In September
1960, the two friends went to New York to meet with Wagman,
and soon Brown and Wagman were giving Moe a pitch, promising him four figures just for flubbing a few shots or laying
down on defense.

Moe and Brown might have been close, Moe said years later, but that friendship wasn't enough to get him to taint a basketball game. Two months after that initial meeting, Moe and
Brown met with Wagman again so that he could tell Wagman
that he would not play ball with the gamblers. But at the first
meeting, Moe did accept $75 that Wagman offered him to re-
imburse him for his trip up North. "I met the guy, he gave me
seventy-five bucks, he said, 'This is for your trip up,'" Moe said.
"So I took the money, put it in my pocket, that was it."

Those meetings occurred at the beginning of Moe's senior
year, and he played clean throughout that season, but he never told Coach Frank McGuire about his meeting with Brown
and Wagman. Every year during the preseason, McGuire
would show his players a scrapbook of clippings from the New
York City scandals in the early fifties, and he would tell them
his expectations: Not only were the players not to enter any
agreements with gamblers, they were to tell the coaches immediately if they were ever approached by a gambler. Moe had
kept the money, and he had kept quiet, and that was enough to
sully his reputation during that period.

Moe had a great deal of respect for Chancellor Aycock, and
when the story about him broke he went to Aycock and admitted accepting the money. Around the same time, Moe signed
a contract with a new NBA team, the Chicago Packers, and he

had two meetings with the team's president to assure him of his innocence in the point-shaving operation. On May 2, the university's Honor Council considered Moe's case and cleared him of violating the school's honor code. But the next day, according to news reports, Aycock kicked him out of school.

It would seem that Moe, just finished with a stellar collegiate career and with professional basketball in his sights, had received unusually harsh punishment when he was asked to leave the University of North Carolina just a month before his class was set to graduate. But the true story, Moe said fifty years later, wasn't nearly as dramatic. The truth was, he was on the verge of failing out of school anyway, and Aycock saw the controversy as an open door to give Moe a second chance. The following fall, because of Aycock's help, Moe enrolled at Elon University, twenty miles east of Chapel Hill.

"I had to leave because I didn't go to class and was failing everything," Moe said. "I was struggling just to be eligible. Chancellor Aycock got me into Elon."

It took two full years of buckling down at Elon, including every summer session, for Moe to earn his degree. The consequences of that $75 lingered when NBA Commissioner Maurice Podoloff refused to let him sign with the Chicago team, citing a strict policy against any player who was known to associate with gamblers. The American Basketball Association, founded in 1967, did want Moe, and he played for five seasons in that league before beginning a thirty-year coaching career first in the ABA and later the NBA when the two leagues merged.

The twists and turns of Moe's story dominated the sports headlines for all of April and part of May, but those close to Everett Case knew that he was uneasy. He couldn't forget what he had seen that night against Georgia Tech, and Wake County's district solicitor Lester Chalmers had been actively looking into the possibility of point-shaving activity in Raleigh ever since Case alerted him to his concerns. The UNC plotline, starring Lou Brown and Doug Moe, finally died down after Moe left UNC in May, but after May 13, 1961, the scandal would seem to exist for all time before a red-and-white background. That afternoon the media was invited to a two o'clock press conference on the N. C. State campus.

The headline on Page 1-A of the *News and Observer* delivered the heart-stopping news in bold one-inch type: "Three N. C. State Players Charged with Cage Fixing." The revelation: The State Bureau of Investigation had uncovered illegal behavior by Muehlbauer, Niewierowski, and Litchfield. Muehlbauer and Litchfield were arrested and held under $3,000 bond, and a warrant was issued for Niewierowski, who was home in New York City at the time, with Raleigh police requesting extradition from New York.

The warrants mentioned four specific games in which Muehlbauer engaged in point shaving, two for Niewierowski, and two for Litchfield, with the Georgia Tech game which initially raised Case's suspicion on the list for both Muehlbauer and Litchfield. Chalmers, a young attorney who was almost single-handedly striving to bring some justice to the situation in Wake County, told the reporter that his investigation might yet yield "another eighteen, twenty-four, or thirty-six indictments." He further promised, "We will investigate every team that has played in the Coliseum."

Reaction to the news ranged from disbelief to sadness to quiet pride in Case as his role in blowing the whistle on his own players came out. North Carolina Governor Terry Sanford called it "a distressing development" and said that he would wait for the Consolidated University of North Carolina Board of Trustees meeting on May 22, when President William Friday would deliver a full report of the events. The Wolfpack players who were unconnected to the gamblers were shocked, and most said that they had few suspicions of their guilty teammates.

Starter Bob DiStefano, who played summer ball in the Catskills but told reporters he was never approached by anyone hoping to buy his cooperation, said that Litchfield surprised him the most, and Muehlbauer was "the type of guy who's easily led." Niewierowski, on the other hand, always loved to place a trivial wager, and he was open about his wish to get rich someday. In Niewierowski's freshman basketball questionnaire, a sheet filled out by all Wolfpack recruits when they arrived on campus, he indicated that his primary future goal was to make money. Two days after the warrant was issued, Niewierowski was taken into custody in New York.

Niewierowski and Muehlbauer had withdrawn from N. C. State a month before the revelations at the request of school officials, apparently because of their failure to attend classes. Niewierowski, like UNC's Doug Moe, had signed a contract with the NBA Chicago Packers. NCSU teammate John Punger speculated that Niewierowski's hopes for a college degree and a future in professional basketball had both disintegrated in the span of that single press conference. "I don't know what he's going to do," Punger lamented to a reporter.

Sports editor Dick Herbert praised his friend Case for his integrity in the tragic episode in his May 14 column, reminding fans how diligent he was each year in educating his players about the dangers of consorting with gamblers. "In what may be its saddest moment in its athletic history, State College can take some consolation from the fact it smelled the rotten odor in its barn and asked the proper authorities to do something about it," Herbert wrote. "In all the other basketball fixes, coaches of the teams involved have been shocked by surprise. They did not have an inkling of what was going on. Everett Case did."

Before his arrest on the day the charges were revealed, Litchfield was ill in the N. C. State infirmary. He told reporter Joe Tiede that he only agreed to cooperate during the Georgia

Tech game, but as it turned out he played very little and he played his best when he was on the floor. He also said he never received any money, since Joe Greene asked the players to return the payments when N. C. State did not make the spread against Georgia Tech. He said that when Case brought in the SBI officers the previous fall, he decided not to be involved with any further games, and his cooperation with the gambling outfit had weighed on his conscience ever since. "I've worried about it almost every night," he admitted.

All over the country, scenes similar to the one in Raleigh were playing out, as players beloved by fans admitted to putting their desire for riches ahead of team interests. But not every Big Four team fell in the scandal's shadow. Vic Bubas, a former player and assistant coach at N. C. State, expressed sadness over the Wolfpack allegations, but none of the athletes on the Duke team he now led were ever sullied in the scandal. The fourth Big Four school was little Wake Forest, which had enjoyed a stretch of glory days recently, capturing trophies in both the Dixie Classic and the ACC Tournament. As exams got under way on campus, one of their most visible stars, former Dixie Classic MVP Billy Packer, found himself embroiled in the controversy because of a curious case of mistaken identity.

Packer was interrupted from studying one day by an emphatic knock on the door. He opened the door to two men in dark suits.

"It's mid-May, and I'm studying for exams, and these two guys come to my room," Packer said. "They say, 'Are you Packer? We need you to come with us.' And they take me to the president's office at Wake Forest. And on the way over there they're saying, 'You know why we're here.' And they were from the New York City District Attorney's office. And I say, 'I have no idea.' And they say, 'Look, kid, we know exactly what you did.' So by the time I get to the president's office, I realize that these guys think I'm involved in the point shaving."

In disbelief, Packer followed the men to the office of Wake Forest President Dr. Harold Tribble. He knew that his shooting had been in a slump in the NCAA East Regional—he averaged only 3.6 points a game during that tournament. Not only that, but several of the old teammates and opponents he had known growing up in Pennsylvania had already been fingered in the fixing scheme. But the officers' stark accusation still came as a shock.

"Dr. Tribble called me in to his office, and he said, 'Now Billy, I'm only going to ask you this one time. Are you in any way involved in this scandal?'" Packer remembered. "I said, 'No. I've never been approached by anybody.'"

Tribble assured Packer that he believed him and that Wake Forest would stand behind him through whatever ensued. The agents told Packer to wait in the office while they went to get one of his teammates who was also under investigation. Packer thought that it had to be Len Chappell, the Demon Deacons' top scorer and the only other player who would really be in a position to alter the outcome of a game. Instead, the plot took yet another unexpected twist when the agents led Jack Jensen into the room.

Jensen was a Wake Forest fan and loyal basketball follower who had been so eager to travel with the team that he had hitchhiked to a few games. McKinney had an extra roster spot, and he liked Jensen's loyalty, so he gave him a jersey and let him travel with the team. Jensen played extremely sparingly, and when Packer saw him he burst out laughing, because he knew Jensen couldn't possibly have been in on a fix. Packer was innocent but he said he was certainly guilty of a failure to respect certain authority figures, especially those who, as he saw it, were so clearly in the wrong.

"Jensen walks in the door, and he's ashen, and I'm laughing," Packer said. "I'm so far out of line as a kid at that time, in terms of attitude, that these guys are pissed off, because they haven't found anybody that would laugh under these circumstances. And Jens is saying, 'I've only gotten to take about three shots in my career. And I try to make all my shots.' And he's panicked. So they let Jensy go, I'm guilty, and they're sending me to New York."

Bones McKinney asked one of his assistants, Charlie Bryant, to accompany Packer to New York City, which was hosting a constant stream of college basketball players in a wide-scale interrogation led by Manhattan District Attorney Frank Hogan. Packer wasn't worried or afraid on his unscheduled trip North; he was actually glad that he would be able to see his girlfriend Barbara, who lived in Philadelphia.

Packer and Bryant had to wait in a spacious room that was full of suspected players from all over the country. One by one they were led back to smaller rooms to face questioning, and some of the young men looked like they were starting to crack under the pressure. "I saw several kids come out and just break down," Bryant said. "One kid went running over and apologized to his mom and dad and threw his arms around them." Packer, though, steadfastly denied ever even talking to gambling interests, and after two days he called Wake Forest to talk to President Tribble, who then got on the phone with one of the agents and demanded that Billy be released and sent back to North Carolina. "Maybe I should have understood the serious nature of it, but I had kind of a good time arguing with them," Packer said.

It was back in Winston-Salem that Packer finally reconciled the agents' shadowy accusations with reality. In New York, he was asked repeatedly about a visitor to his hotel room on the night after Wake Forest defeated St. John's in the NCAA Regional. With Tribble acting as a middleman, the detectives revealed that they suspected Packer had received a late-night visit from Jack Molinas, the mastermind of the entire point-shaving operation. Packer racked his brain for an explanation, and finally remembered his friend Dick Markowitz, who had stopped by looking for an empty bed when he missed his team bus back to George Washington University. Suddenly it all added up, even the inclusion of Jensen, because Packer sent Markowitz to Jensen's room that night to sleep.

"Markowitz looked like Jack Molinas—the same size, the same kind of clothes and so forth—so they think it's Molinas who has come to my room," Packer said, remembering Markowitz's snappy dressing, dark features, and ever-present fedora.

Tribble and Packer called the agents in New York and told them about Markowitz, and they tracked him down and corroborated Packer's story. But it was only after several more insistent phone calls from the university president to the detectives that Packer was finally cleared. Decades later Packer remained convinced that if he had chosen to play basketball at a different college, his name might have been forever sullied by an association with that scandal.

"Dr. Tribble said, 'Billy Packer has been to New York, he's been investigated, he claims that he has nothing to do with this, and Wake Forest stands behind him.' It was the only school in the United States who defended any of their players."

Fourteen

As a parade of terrified college hoops players was being summoned to New York for questioning by District Attorney Frank Hogan and his staff, the implicated N. C. State athletes awaited trial in Wake County, home to Raleigh. But they had already been excommunicated from the university that welcomed them South from New York a few years earlier, brimming with talent and promise.

By the time the charges against Stan Niewierowski, Anton Muehlbauer, and Terry Litchfield were revealed on May 14, Niewierowski and Muehlbauer had already withdrawn from NCSU, according to a statement from Chancellor John Caldwell, and they would not be permitted to return. Litchfield, who like Muehlbauer would have had one more year of basketball eligibility remaining, was permanently dismissed from the team and the university.

Soon Niewierowski was in custody in New York and Muehlbauer was held briefly in the Wake County jail and then released on bail. Litchfield was sleeping in the N. C. State infirmary when the charges were revealed, and he was under house arrest there while he recuperated from a sore throat and a fever. All three were silent when reached by reporters, but Litchfield's father, who was the executive director of the Kentucky YMCA, did sit down to talk about his son when he came to town; about his improbable basketball success despite such severe visual impairment that his parents were once told he was blind and he had to attend a special school for much of his childhood.

"I guess [the gamblers] hit him when he was at his low point," Alfred Litchfield told a writer from the UPI. "It could have happened to anyone his age. He's got a tremendous adjustment to make now. He doesn't know how much. None of the boys involved realize what life is going to be like for them after this."

While the three Wolfpack players and their families tried to navigate the murky waters of consequence, one former teammate's name was conspicuously absent from every report of point shaving. Don Gallagher was a decorated athlete and student when he graduated in the spring of 1960, and he rode that success into service in the U.S. Army. He was sent on a tour of duty in West Germany, but even in Europe he could not escape reports that his former teammates were being fingered for fixing games. He was burdened with guilt and with fear that his involvement would inevitably come to light. It took four months, but on September 12, 1961, working from the testimony of the other players, the Wake County grand jury finally named Gallagher as a conspirator.

It was a period of uncertainty for everybody—basketball players who faced the real possibility of jail time, fans who were devastated by the breach of trust from athletes who had represented their beloved teams, and coaches who were up nights wondering if they could have done more to prevent their players' association with unsavory people. For N.C. State assistant coach Lee Terrill, the revelations were the end of a promising coaching career, according to his widow Pat. She recalled one night during that time when Everett Case, her husband Lee, and a few other friends sat up late discussing the fixes and lamenting the quick decline of the game that had given them all so many gratifying moments.

About her husband, Pat Terrill remembered, "He said that to put so much trust in these young men, and to feel so close to them and to have this happen, he felt betrayed. He felt he couldn't in good faith continue to recruit young men. I'm sure he would have gone on to be a good coach somewhere else." Instead, Terrill, who passed away in 1988, transitioned to the business world and had a successful career with the Eastman Chemical Company.

The coaches might have felt the most disillusionment in the wake of the scandals, but the man who was under the most pressure that May was William Friday. It was incumbent on the forty-year-old college administrator to respond appropriately to the allegations that were, some feared, serious enough to sound a death knell for college basketball in Big Four country.

Even though Friday was young, it wasn't the first time his leadership mettle had been tested. Like most men of his generation, he had been in the military during World War II, serving as a weapons analyst at the U.S. Navy Ammunition and Weapons Center in Norfolk, Virginia. Three years after the war ended, Friday stepped into his first leadership post in higher education, as the assistant dean of students at the University of North Carolina. From there he became the assistant to Gordon Gray, the president of the Consolidated University of North Carolina. In 1956, when he was just thirty-six, Friday was asked to take over when Gray stepped down from the post, and what followed was a thirty-year tenure as the system president that many believe made him the most influential figure ever in North Carolina higher education.

Friday was troubled by the trends that seemed to accompany the rise of college basketball as a national spectator sport. Many players were being given scholarships without regard to their academic fitness, and coaches in North Carolina and elsewhere were running afoul of the NCAA because of questionable recruiting practices. By early 1961, N.C. State had already been disciplined by college athletics' governing body twice and the University of North Carolina had been put on probation once.

The episode that left the bitterest taste in Friday's mouth was the Jackie Moreland case in 1956, in which Case and his staff had been sanctioned by the NCAA for a list of recruiting infractions, namely offering to pay for the player's girlfriend's education as well as proffering $1,000 a year to Moreland. No Wolfpack coach or booster ever admitted to the most egregious of the allegations, and even though the NCAA levied a four-year suspension the officials in that organization would not reveal their findings to Friday. He was responsible for both the University of North Carolina and N.C. State, and he had given those two chancellors authority to deal with athletic issues early in his term as president, but still he felt like he had been shut out in the Moreland case.

"Thoroughly disgusted with the NCAA style of investigation, he was also suspicious of the State College sports establishment while fully cognizant of the entrenched alumni and commercial interests that surrounded it," wrote Bill Link in William Friday's biography. "Moreover, Friday realized that uncontrolled intercollegiate sports threatened a university's academic integrity. All these considerations convinced Friday that if he were to face another issue of administrative control over intercollegiate athletics less equivocal than the Moreland case, he would act decisively."

It was five years before that next issue rolled into Friday's territory, and it came in the form of the point-shaving operation being directed by Jack Molinas in New York City. He was disheartened as he learned about the players from North Carolina and N.C. State who had engaged in illegal activity. The low point for Friday—and the moment that prodded him into decisive action—came in a conversation with district solicitor Lester Chalmers. One Saturday morning that May, Chalmers called and set up an appointment in Friday's Chapel Hill office.

"He said, 'I've got to tell you that these gamblers stuck a gun in the stomach of these athletes and said, "Give me back the money," when the game throwing didn't work out,'" Friday said. "When a kid's life is threatened—and I know it was threatened, and the district attorney did, or he wouldn't have been here—you had to eliminate the problem."

An episode similar to the one Chalmers described had happened to Don Gallagher in early 1960, but his name had not surfaced yet that spring. However, the Wake County investigators had heard of similar threats made to other players, likely those involved with the Georgia Tech game in November 1961. The players who were paid to fix that contest had failed to cover the point spread, and they were forced to give the money back to the gambling operatives. Although it was never reported which player testified that a gambler pointed a gun at his stomach, that story was more than enough for Friday. The situation was grave, and the consequences needed to reflect that. "Friday himself was determined to administer bitter medicine," Link wrote in Friday's biography. "He realized, along with the chancellors, that the situation had reached a desperate point when gamblers were themselves visiting Reynolds Coliseum and dealing directly with student athletes."

Friday had promised a statement on the point-shaving incidents at the scheduled May 22 meeting of the Consolidated University's board of trustees, and in the days before that meeting he spent hours behind closed doors with the two chancellors, William Aycock from the University of North Carolina and John Caldwell from N. C. State. Friday observed a strict information blackout during this time, even steering clear of his old friend Dick Herbert from the Raleigh *News and Observer*.

"I asked for a meeting of the board of trustees, but I didn't tell anybody what I was going to do until I got in there," Friday said. "And Dick Herbert was one of my very best friends, he was sports editor of the *News and Observer*. He called me the night before, and he said, 'What are you going to do?' and I said, 'Dick, I can't tell you.' And he became very angry with me. But I knew all I had to do was let that leak and then I could never get it done."

In the week before the meeting, Herbert speculated in his daily column about the penalties that could be forthcoming. Having heard university officials and others throw around the word "de-emphasis," Herbert took the position that while wayward individuals on teams needed to face strict consequences, the basketball programs themselves should not be in anyone's crosshairs. "De-emphasis is not the proper approach," he wrote. "Instead there should be a determined effort to establish sound policies and see that they stick." Also that week, Everett Case surprised the Wolfpack Nation with his statement that schools like N. C. State should limit out-of-state recruiting, since all of the players involved with the scandal were from New York and had connections with gambling interests in the East.

As the three educators hashed out ways to bring basketball into its proper place under the academic mission of the universities, they discussed a number of practices that they believed to be representative of the tail wagging the dog: out-of-state recruiting, lack of academic accountability, and schedules that included too many games, too much travel, and competition during times when school was not even in session. This last factor brought the conversation around to the Dixie Classic. Friday was ready to act drastically, and he believed that abolishing the tournament would speak more loudly than any other restrictions they could dictate. The chancellors had mixed feelings. For Caldwell at N. C. State, the Classic was a moneymaker and a publicity boon, and his community had the most to lose. Aycock, as he told the story nearly forty years later, wasn't as attached to the event.

"It was not a difficult decision, especially for me, because I didn't care anything about the Dixie Classic to begin with,"

Aycock told author Bill Link in a 1999 interview. "We were just one of the eight participants. The Dixie Classic was on the State College campus, and it was a State College tournament envisioned by Coach Case."

Later, Caldwell would say that he believed Friday would only suspend the Dixie Classic for one year, not permanently. But as Friday remembered it years later, the three men were in agreement as they drafted the lengthy resolution to present to the board of trustees. They agreed that they had the authority to make decisions without the board's approval. The final word would be Friday's, and he knew that he would need to stand steadfastly behind any changes he proposed. "We agreed that we wouldn't ask the board to decide, because I had the authority," Friday said. And in 1999 he told Link, "If I had turned the things over to the trustees, I think we'd probably have had four meetings, six committees, and never gotten to the decision point."

Shortly after eleven on May 22, the trustees gathered in the N.C. State Student Union. Friday, always a man of action, wasted no time in handing out a seven-page statement, which he then read to the board. It took him more than fifteen minutes.

"I come now to the subject of recent prominence: namely, basketball," Friday began. "These events have caused us serious embarrassment. They have administered a new shock in a part of college life where we have come dangerously close to being shock-proof. But we determined to take action that would be clear in its purpose and specific in its application, and we have done so."

Next, Friday reminded the trustees of their decision, years earlier, to place athletic matters in the hands of the chancellors and the system president. He then presented a brief history of the events which had nudged him to this point: NCSU's first probation in 1954, the Moreland imbroglio in 1956, the

UNC probation that January, and the series of dominoes that led to the revelation of widespread point-shaving at the two universities.

He assured the board of his resolve "to counter scandal with saving remedies," then presented two basic courses of action that he and the chancellors considered to that end. The first was to discontinue altogether or suspend the basketball programs at the two schools, and the second was to continue basketball competition, but "move forthrightly to eliminate or correct conditions that have discredited the sport." Then, with that lengthy introduction behind him, Friday unveiled three major reforms for the basketball teams at N. C. State and the University of North Carolina.

First, because some of the fixers had been contacted by gambling interests while playing in a summer league in the Catskills, Friday instituted a ban on all organized basketball during the summer. This prohibition was later adopted by the NCAA for players at all schools. Second, Friday made an official policy regarding out-of-state recruiting, echoing the convictions that had been recently voiced by Case. Starting with the fresh-man class of 1962, the institutions would only be allowed to give two scholarships to players from outside the Atlantic Coast Conference area, a restriction that would also apply to football.

The third change, which would lead to the bombshell that reverberated in the ears of basketball fans for years, involved trimming the schedule to include only the fourteen required ACC contests, the ACC tournament, the NCAA tournament if a team qualified, and no more than two games from outside the conference. Since every team in the Dixie Classic played three games, this last restriction was the handwriting on the wall for the beloved tournament, but Friday went on in clearer terms.

"Among other things, this means the immediate discon-tinuance of the Dixie Classic," he said. "Holiday tournaments, of which the Dixie Classic is a prominent example, conducted at a time when college is not in session, exemplify the exploitation for public entertainment or for budgetary and commercial purposes of a sports program which properly exists as an adjunct to collegiate education. These tournaments subject the students, the coaches, and the colleges to unnecessary demands and unwise distractions."

In a moment, in a student union meeting room in late May, the Dixie Classic was no more. It was the last penalty outlined by Friday, but for days afterward it was the first thing on the lips of sports fans and in the headlines of papers around the South. Herbert called the ban "the hardest blow of all" and conjectured that top players would no longer choose to play at the schools because of the severe curtailment of their schedule. Coaches from around the country weighed in on the decision, and two ACC-member coaches from outside North Carolina—Bob Stevens from South Carolina and Bill McCann from Virginia—said that the moves would weaken their conference, which prior to the revelations had been on the rise nationally.

"This is bound to lower the prestige of the ACC," McCann warned. "Eventually, it will really hurt basketball at Carolina and State and it will hurt the rest of us too. I think the decision is entirely wrong."

Many concurred with that opinion, but Case was mostly quiet with the press and respectful of the rulings made by his superiors. After the decisions were announced, he gathered his team together to discuss the repercussions. Squad member Les Robinson remembered that the coach was surprisingly optimistic about what the future held, despite the abolition of his beloved tournament and the drastic changes in scheduling and recruiting. As they gathered in a classroom in Reynolds, Case gave each of the players a copy of his public statement on the matter, and while he admitted that major adjustments were ahead, he tried to cast it as a positive.

"He said it will be less travel, more study time, miss less classes, and we've just got to work hard and work around this," Robinson said. "Just a real positive outlook."

Later that year, when the holidays drew near and Case started considering what type of Christmas card he might send, his lingering feelings about the end of the Classic were made clear. He commissioned Bill Ballard, a talented sports cartoonist for the *News and Observer* whose detailed representations of the tournament ran in the paper before each Dixie Classic, to draw his card that year. The cover showed Santa Claus on his sleigh, flying over an empty Reynolds Coliseum and saying, "Hmmmm ... that's strange, the place is empty, and it used to be a regular stop. Oh well, Merry Christmas wherever you are!" The inside of the card depicted a lone wolf sitting in an otherwise deserted arena, saying, "Yeah, and a Ho-Ho-Ho." To Robinson, who received one of the cards, it told the poignant story about how the coach was greeting his first holiday season since 1949 without a Dixie Classic.

As Friday and the university system exacted their sentence on players, coaches, and fans alike, law enforcement officers and investigators were consumed with peeling back the many layers of a point-shaving network that extended from coast to coast. On May 25, twelve more players were implicated, but none were from Big Four schools. On the home front, the man who was at the vortex of the inquiry was the determined young lawyer Lester Chalmers.

Chalmers was a Raleigh native who had set his sights on becoming a lawyer from a very young age, but he also loved watching and playing sports. He was talented enough at football that he had originally hoped to earn a football scholarship to fund his college education, but that course was forever altered when Pearl Harbor was attacked during his senior year in high school. Within months, Chalmers had shifted his focus from touchdowns to defending the Pacific theater from

Japanese invaders. While he was still a teenager, Chalmers saw fierce battles as part of a PT boat crew under General Douglas MacArthur.

Like Bill Friday, Chalmers displayed a degree of courage and confidence in his chosen field that belied his young age. In his early thirties when he was first appointed as the Wake County district solicitor and just thirty-six when he began his investigation of the point-shaving activity, Chalmers was always unmoved by public criticism of the causes he championed. In the Pacific, he had battled genuine enemies and seen brave men die in that pursuit. As his widow Alta saw it, the clamor over a basketball tournament's cancellation could not possibly wound him. "He had seen things," she said.

After Everett Case's first visit to report the suspicious N. C. State-Georgia Tech game, Chalmers became fixed on discovering the truth. He began a long process of talking to anyone in gambling or basketball circles who might have some information that would either exonerate or implicate the players from N. C. State. He also developed a close working relationship with the New York City detectives who were looking into the fixes under the direction of Manhattan's district attorney Frank Hogan.

Chalmers's son Tim was only nine years old when a group of New York detectives came to his Raleigh home to meet with his father, but he would long carry with him a memory of their guns. Each of the detectives had a gun on his belt, but the image that was most indelible to Tim was that of the smaller pistol each man had strapped to his ankle. It was clear that this was serious business. That spring, Chalmers also made several visits to New York to meet with investigators and to assess the progress of the court proceedings against some of the conspirators.

The mood in the sports community was one of fearful anticipation; everyone dreaded that their favorite team or player might be the next one named, and a flurry of rumors further fed the paranoia. In an interview with Dick Herbert on May 23, Chalmers asked fans to reserve judgment and wait for the proceedings to play out.

"I urge the public not to circulate rumors," he said. "Almost all of them are unfounded. A number of people are being hurt unjustly by the talk that is going around. We realize this and would like to bring all of it to an end as quickly as possible."

Today's image of a district attorney farming out cases to his staff bears no resemblance to the Wake County office in Chalmers's day. District solicitor was a part-time job; he had to practice in a private law office just to make enough money to support his family. He also had a part-time assistant, but most of the big cases he tackled in those days fell squarely on his shoulders. Chalmers showed singular focus in talking to every involved player about each detail of their conversations with the men in the gambling network, because he understood that identifying the fixers on the court only uncovered the first layer of the deception that had been practiced on the American basketball fan. Chalmers's ultimate goal was to demand accountability from the men who had controlled the money and enticed young athletes to sell out at schools across the nation.

May unfolded with the naming of more guilty players—at UCLA, at Dayton, at Bradley—but Chalmers continued to burrow down to the deeper levels of the cases in his purview. Before long, he had learned enough detail from the N. C. State and North Carolina players to issue his first Wake County warrants targeted at the gamblers themselves. In May, warrants were issued for Joe Greene and Lou Barshak, both of New York, and on June 4, Chalmers also issued warrants against Aaron Wagman and Bob Kraw, also of New York. He promised more warrants the following week.

In New York, Jack Molinas was still playing in East Coast basketball tournaments and working all of the angles in his extensive gambling pipeline, even while his close associate Joe Hacken and a half dozen of his other deputies sat in jail due to point-shaving charges. Molinas had gone to great lengths to farm out the actual contact with the athletes to men like Joe Greene, and he was counting on the loyalty of his close friends in the network, so Molinas moved through that spring as if he was still untouchable. Even Ray Paprocky, a New York University player who had been targeted for recruitment by Molinas and Hacken because of his financial woes and later collected $2,300 for fixing games, told the New York media that May: "They'll never get the big guys." From his small office in Raleigh, Lester Chalmers was determined to prove Paprocky wrong.

Fifteen

Alta Chalmers did not see much of her husband in late 1961 and early 1962. Lester Chalmers was juggling his many duties as Wake County district solicitor and in private law while devoting any spare moments to the investigation into basketball point-shaving. He was determined to ferret out the truth, but his quest was an isolated one. The hoops-loving Raleigh community, still smarting from William Friday's Dixie Classic death knell in May, was often less than supportive of Chalmers's efforts.

"That was big business here, and it was the social thing," Alta Chalmers said of the tournament. "I don't mean [the opposition] was out in the open, but you got the feeling, they wanted things done, but 'let's don't break up the Dixie Classic.'"

The 1961 point-shaving scandal, with Jack Molinas pulling many of the strings, would ultimately blacken the names of more than fifty college ballplayers from twenty-seven colleges in twenty-two states. But most of those states took little or no legal action against the guilty parties, relying instead on the widespread New York inquiry of Manhattan district attorney Frank Hogan. In South Carolina, for example, at least four players were implicated during later testimony in Wake County, but South Carolina officials never pursued any charges against the players or their gambling connections.

As Chalmers constructed his case, Everett Case prepared for a season that would be marked by the absence of the Dixie

Classic and the weight of Friday's new recruiting and scheduling guidelines. Players like Billy Packer at Wake Forest, who had excelled at past Classics, and Les Robinson at N. C. State, who had relished the thought of taking the court for his first Classic that December, instead resigned themselves to a holiday at home. Tremors from the momentous board of trustees meeting rumbled occasionally that spring, usually in the form of legislators promising to fight for the reinstatement of the Dixie Classic. Twice such resolutions were introduced, but they both failed, and many of the lawmakers and editorial writers who had embraced the tournament in the past suddenly seemed to be swayed by Friday's position.

"It quieted down a good bit," Friday said of the months after he announced his decision. "And we were more sensible about it, not because of the decision so much as people began to realize what we'd done, the gravity of it. And by that, I mean the threat to human life. We've had other scandals in sports, but nothing like that one, nothing with threatening human life."

It was August before another domino fell, and this time the rumbling came not from Raleigh but from Chapel Hill. After nine years at the helm of the UNC squad, Frank McGuire left to take the head coaching position with the Philadelphia Warriors of the NBA. (After just one season in Philadelphia, McGuire returned south for a fifteen-year stint as the head coach at the University of South Carolina.)

The involvement of Tar Heel players in the fixes certainly had some bearing on McGuire's departure, but insiders had long known that he was dissatisfied with the way he was treated by the university's administration and that he felt his program was never sufficiently rewarded for its 1957 undefeated national championship season. McGuire's most determined battle, which was fruitless despite his efforts, was for the construction of a new arena to replace Woollen Gym, which seated only 6,000 and featured a leaky roof.

McGuire's replacement was a little-known assistant coach named Dean Smith, who had come to North Carolina in 1958 as the Tar Heels' freshman coach and was promoted to the top job in the fall of 1961 when McGuire stepped down. Smith, who was famously burned in effigy by disgruntled fans during that first season, went on to become the winningest coach in school history and number three on the all-time national victories list. In the same year that William Friday announced his plan to de-emphasize basketball in North Carolina public universities, the school where Friday's office was housed hired the coach that would go on to bring unparalleled glory to the UNC program.

"My joke always is, that de-emphasis really worked on North Carolina and North Carolina State basketball—six national championships later," said Les Robinson, referring to the UNC national titles in 1982, 1993, 2005, and 2009, and the championships won by N. C. State in 1974 and 1983.

It wasn't until late 1962, as Smith was starting his second year leading the Tar Heels and Case was beginning what would be a difficult 10–11 season, when the trials of the gamblers involved in the North Carolina point-shaving scandals finally opened at the Wake County courthouse. The proceedings began on November 19, and before they concluded six different men would have either pleaded "no contest" or been convicted on bribery charges related to the ten N. C. State games that were allegedly fixed between 1959 and 1961.

The six gambling operatives who appeared in the Wake County court that fall were Joe Greene, who had made the initial contact with Don Gallagher at the Catskills; Dave Goldberg, who took Gallagher for a threatening walk following a botched Duke fix in early 1960; Steve Lekometros, an associate of Goldberg's from St. Louis; and three New York men named Michael Siegal, Lou Barshak, and Paul Walker, who had been found by Chalmers to have some culpability in the scheme. Nine other men were named in Chalmers's indictments but never testified in North Carolina due to similar proceedings against them in other states. One of those, who was on trial in New York at the same time Chalmers was calling witnesses in Raleigh, was Jack Molinas.

A lifetime of treachery and greed had finally caught up to Molinas. A Toledo basketball player named Billy Reed, under the direction of Frank Hogan and his staff, had recorded a conversation with Molinas in which Molinas talked about his involvement in the point-shaving operation. Molinas was charged and arrested, and his trial began on October 30, 1962. Before jury selection began, he was offered a deal, which would have resulted in a six-month sentence and the revocation of his law license if he would confess to masterminding a few fixes. He refused, choosing instead to defend his avowed innocence in court. According to a New York reporter on the first day of the trial, Molinas, ever the huckster, sidled up to District Attorney Hogan and said, "I'll bet you ten thousand dollars that you won't convict me."

After a month of testimony, Molinas's New York trial was recessed because the judge fell ill, and it did not resume for more than a month. On December 6, according to Charley Rosen's book about Molinas, the gambler asked to see a reporter's newspaper so that he could check on the trial that was underway in North Carolina. He learned that the defendants had already been found guilty of bribery, with sentencing scheduled for the following day. "They sure do things fast down there," Molinas commented to the reporter. "I hope my jury doesn't read about this case."

During the North Carolina proceedings, with Judge Herman Clark presiding, Lieutenant Don Gallagher, cutting a striking figure in his army uniform, took the stand to recount the details of his dealings with the gambling network. After his name finally surfaced in September, Gallagher received a subpoena while serving in West Germany, and along with Niewierowski, Muehlbauer, Litchfield, and Lou Brown from UNC, he was granted immunity in both New York and North Carolina in exchange for his testimony against the men who had engineered the fixes. Courtroom observers were rapt as from the witness stand Gallagher recounted the story of the night Goldberg and Greene paid him a late-night visit to express their dissatisfaction about his failure to hold up his end of the deal.

As they walked down a dark Raleigh street that night, Gallagher testified, Goldberg told him, 'If you're a nice guy, you should stay out of this thing. You shouldn't be involved." He also recalled his apprehension when Greene came to his door and warned him that someone in Goldberg's car had a gun: "I didn't have any intention of getting shot," he said. "I wanted to keep somebody between me and the car."

Another memorable day of testimony came from Joe Greene, who was the first contact for Gallagher and Niewierowski and was himself a codefendant in Chalmers's case. Greene had entered a guilty plea and took a reduced sentence in return for testifying. He had come to North Carolina from imprisonment in a Manhattan jail called The Tombs, but he was still awaiting sentencing in New York. On October 4, while out on bail, he had swallowed a bottle of sleeping pills, and when that suicide attempt failed he slashed his wrists with a razor blade. His bail was revoked and he was sent to The Tombs, where he was held as a star witness for the trials in both New York and North Carolina.

When he appeared before Judge Clark in Wake County, Greene appeared "gaunt and nervous on the witness stand," reported the *News and Observer,* and he told the jury that he had worked on fixes that were funded by Goldberg and Lekemetros. The confrontation with Gallagher came about because the two St. Louis men were afraid that the scheme might be flimsy, and they threatened to take their money elsewhere. At one point that evening, before they visited Gallagher's apartment, Lekemetros told Greene, "I think I smell a rat."

Defense attorney William Hatch also quizzed Greene about the charges pending against him in New York and his recent attempts to end his life. "I felt like I did a lot of damage to a great number of people and would have to continue to do damage to other people," he explained. A former New York basketball standout himself, Greene said that he was offered a scholarship to the University of Cincinnati years before but the offer was withdrawn when he was found to be academically ineligible.

"You could not qualify, so you got mad with basketball and everybody who played it," Hatch said.

Greene responded that he had been disappointed when the scholarship fell through.

"You set about to destroy the game?" Hatch asked.

"No," answered Greene, and *News and Observer* writer Charles Craven reported that with that reply he smiled for the first time during the questioning.

Neither Gallagher nor Greene's testimonies lacked drama, but no presence on the stand was as heart-wrenching for observers as that of Everett Case, who had personally set the tempest spinning when he turned in his own team after that fateful game against Georgia Tech. Charlie Bryant, a friend and assistant coach of Case's in his later years at N.C. State, said that Case's life "was almost one hundred percent basketball." Using materials like winning seasons, spectacular players, and an unparalleled holiday tournament, Case had constructed a spectacular monument to basketball in the state of North Carolina. That day he was called to a Raleigh courtroom to speak words which could severely damage that legacy.

The chief theme of Case's testimony was the 1960 Georgia Tech game that set a series of alarming revelations into motion.

Case testified that he was anxious going into that contest because the Yellow Jackets had beaten the Wolfpack soundly in their last meeting, and he was looking for a decisive victory in response. "I think at one time we had a 17- to 18-point lead with eight to ten minutes to play," he said. But that large lead evaporated quickly, with State ultimately only prevailing by six points, and it was during the later minutes of the game that Case saw mistakes that seemed uncharacteristic of his players.

Just before Case took the stand, Terry Litchfield and Anton Muehlbauer, players who had once vowed to represent the Wolfpack and compete the Case way, testified about their involvement in the attempted fix of that Georgia Tech game. They exceeded the spread that the gamblers were counting on, they told the court, so both men had returned the money to the gambling operative who had contacted them, a New Yorker named Bob Kraw. The fix failed, but Case's suspicions were aroused and the damage was done. That December, Lester Chalmers and his colleague Frank Hogan in New York would see justice for the "big guys" who had wielded the most influence in the massive scheme.

Goldberg and Lekemetros, the only two men named in Chalmers's indictment who did not plead guilty and agree to a settlement, were each sentenced to five years in a North Carolina prison and a $30,000 fine. The conspirators who pled guilty were given anywhere from eighteen months in prison to suspended sentences, depending on their prior convictions and their level of involvement.

In New York, Greene was given a prison sentence of six to seven years, to be served after an extensive psychiatric examination. The most severe penalty handed to any of Molinas's associates prior to February 1963 was the eight-year sentence given to his close friend Joe Hacken in a separate New York trial.

In Manhattan on January 7, Jack Molinas was found guilty on three counts of bribery involving specific games and two counts of "attempted subornation of perjury and conspiracy to fix twenty-five other games involving twenty-two players from twelve colleges." His sentencing was scheduled for February 11, and that day the New York assistant district attorney asked the judge to impose the maximum sentence for his charges, which would be thirty-five years in prison. Molinas told friends beforehand that he expected his sentence to be comparable to Hacken's eight years, because Hacken had prior arrests.

The sentencing testimony concluded and the judge stood to give his recommendation. Molinas heard his words—two consecutive sentences of five to seven-and-a-half years—but he said in an interview later that he was sure he misunderstood the judge. The sentence of ten to fifteen years, with no possibility of parole for more than six years, was far above anything Molinas or his friends had anticipated. It was also the most severe penalty ever given in New York in a point-shaving case.

Molinas actually served about five-and-a-half years, hastening his parole because of cooperative testimony in another gambling trial. He was released in July 1968, and soon he was placing bets on sporting events again and pursuing a string of shady business deals. His schemes soon brought him to Southern California, where he borrowed money from both powerful Mafia men and Mob-backed Las Vegas casinos. Before long, Molinas, still expecting to slip unscathed through any swindle, had so angered the Mafia that his name was on the agenda of a 1975 meeting of high-level Mob bosses from across the country. After outlining Molinas's various offenses, those assembled took a vote and unanimously decided on "termination."

Jack Molinas was shot to death by a Mob hit man on the patio of his Los Angeles home on August 3, 1975, after he stepped outside with a female friend to admire the view. He was forty-three years old.

With their thirst for riches at the expense of a sport played by college students, Molinas and his operatives had extinguished the dreams of dozens of basketball players. The NBA was no longer a possibility for anyone indicted in the fixes, and the guilty players were immediately *personae non grata* on the campuses that had once embraced them as athletic heroes. Unlike the 1951 New York City scandal, none of the players went to jail this time. But because of an impulsive grab for what seemed like easy money earned on a basketball court, their lives would never be the same. Stanley Cohen, in his book about the New York episode, sketched a stirring picture of this swift fall from grace:

"Culture heroes in their teens, by the time they turned twenty they would be part of the dark side of American folklore," Cohen wrote in *The Game They Played*.

> And it would not be short-lived. Twenty-five years later their telephone numbers would still be unlisted. They were to learn something soon about one of life's fundamental truths, as relentless as it is just: that the past is not neutral; it takes revenge.
>
> Had the players been guilty of a more conventional offense—a crime against person or property; a stolen car, a burglary, a simple assault—redemption no doubt would have come more quickly, more completely, and with less pain. But they had trespassed instead against something far holier than property. They had tampered with childhood ideals, and who among us would not sooner surrender his wallet than his trust? So the price extracted would be great indeed, greater than the jail terms some of them served, greater even than the lost chance to play professional basketball. The steepest price of all was that no one would ever forget.

Les Robinson counted Niewierowski, Muehlbauer, and Litchfield among his friends, and he was one of the few in the

N. C. State family who had any contact with the men after their indictments. Once, after a Wolfpack game in which he played around the time of the trial, Robinson saw Niewierowski in the shadows of a Raleigh apartment complex parking lot. Niewierowski told him that he had attended the game that night, and he complimented Robinson on his play. He had slipped in incognito, stayed in the back, and left before the game ended. Years later, when Robinson was coaching basketball for The Citadel in Charleston, South Carolina, Litchfield called him and told him he was in town for business. Robinson invited him to come visit the gym where he was leading a basketball camp, but Litchfield declined. He told his old friend that he thought it would be better for him if the two were not seen together on a basketball court.

The shine on Wolfpack basketball might have been dulled by the events of early 1961, and four men who once wore N. C. State jerseys might be forever absent from alumni games or homecoming parties, but the Old Gray Fox was still holding court in Reynolds Coliseum. By plowing through the workaday tasks of a coach, Everett Case was doing his best to recapture the glory that had shadowed his program just a few years earlier. His spirit came through in a letter he wrote to one of his players, Smedes York, just before a new season began in October 1962.

"All should report in good condition," Case wrote. "Those of you who do not report in good condition will probably be sitting on the bench or your tongues will be hanging out for awhile ... We can have a good basketball club this season if every one of you make the proper sacrifices and do what is expected of you. This is so vital to the success of any good organization. We are going to start out next Monday, and we are going to be rough and tough. You had better be ready."

He was always quick with an encouraging word for a player, but those who knew Case best noticed that his drive and excitement for the game were somewhat deflated after the scandals. Players, assistants, and fans saw flashes of the old Everett in those final coaching years, but everyone knew something had changed. Prior to the 1962–63 season he hired Press Maravich away from Clemson to be his top assistant and the N. C. State head-coach-in-waiting. Case was in his early sixties and in declining health, and years earlier he had predicted that 1965 would be his last season. He was already suffering with shingles and gout, and the same year he brought Maravich on, he was diagnosed with multiple myeloma, cancer of the bone marrow.

Case continued on for two more seasons after his diagnosis, trudging through a 1963–64 campaign, still shortened by probation from the point-shaving scandals, that ended 8–11, his worst record in eighteen years at N. C. State. Maravich and fellow assistant coach Charlie Bryant became increasingly concerned that the game which had always infused him with life was now hastening his decline. Before the season opener in late 1964, Maravich approached him and told him that he thought Case was letting the game kill him, and the time might be right to step down.

Two games into that season, after an 86–80 road loss to Wake Forest, Case convened an impromptu meeting with his assistants in the shower room at WFU's Memorial Coliseum. Through labored breaths, he told Maravich and Bryant that they needed to take over the team. (Ironically, 1964–65 was also Bones McKinney's final season at Wake Forest. He retired, citing his desire to spend more time with his family, but his hand had been forced by Wake Forest administrators who were concerned about an addiction to alcohol and amphetamines fueled by the long hours and stress of the coaching grind.)

Mindful that Case was surrendering the centerpiece of his life, Maravich asked him to sleep on it. The next morning at six, Case called Maravich with the same message. He was done.

Earlier that year, when Case missed a game against UNC because his illness forced him to be hospitalized, sportswriter Irwin Smallwood, covering the game in Chapel Hill, wrote an open letter to the Old Gray Fox in his newspaper, the Greensboro *Daily News*. "We could tell by the names on the uniforms that State and Carolina were playing tonight, but somehow it wasn't the same," Smallwood's column read. "State without you is like grits and no gravy." Smallwood went on to recall his days as a student sports editor at UNC, when a 1948 contest between N. C. State and UNC attracted such a swarm of fans that the fire marshal called off the game.

"You know, Everett, things have never been the same since that night you and Carolina got 'crowded out,'" Smallwood continued. "Back then, people didn't start talking basketball until Christmas, really. Now, by Thanksgiving, a lot of games are getting close to selling out. The lousy games today draw more than the big games before you came along. Nobody can remember when a game over here hasn't jammed Woollen Gymnasium, and they are building a big addition to the place.

"And it's all because of you."

After his official retirement in December of 1964, even the sagest sports scribes searched for fitting words to pay tribute to the coach who had so elevated the sport of basketball in Raleigh and beyond. Bruce Phillips, the sports editor of the Raleigh *Times*, echoed the feelings of many in the Wolfpack Nation when he wrote, "You knew it was coming, but you dreaded it like the monthly visit to the dentist. The knowledge that Everett Case was throwing off the basketball coaching cloak at N. C. State was common to everyone. But for it to happen so suddenly, well, it buckled the knees from right under you."

Case surrendered the helm of the Wolfpack program with a career record of 377–134. In a fitting tribute to its mentor, the N. C. State squad went on a roll that season, finishing 21–5 and upsetting eighth-ranked Duke in the ACC Tournament final. Case was watching the victory from press row in Reynolds Coliseum, the grand building that if not for him might have been just another typical basketball arena. When his Wolfpack pulled through, the players rushed over to Case, put him on their shoulders and carried him over to cut down the nets one final time.

He was hospitalized again in April of 1965 after breaking a hip on a trip to Las Vegas, and then in July of that year he underwent a major operation to relieve pressure on his spinal cord. By the end of 1965 he was confined to a wheelchair but still greeting streams of friends to his Raleigh home. One of those guests, in December, was John Wooden, the legendary UCLA head coach who had won the second of his national championships the previous spring. Wooden and Case went way back to Indiana, when Wooden's Martinsville High team had played against the Frankfort High team coached by Case.

Case's last visit to Reynolds Coliseum came on December 30, 1965, for a game between N. C. State and West Virginia. It was a date, just before New Year's Eve, when five years earlier his beloved Dixie Classic would have been in full swing, but that night featured a regular game that ended in a 94–77 Wolfpack victory. Before tip-off, Reynolds announcer C. A. Dillon said, "Folks, we're glad to have with us tonight Coach Everett Case." The crowd erupted in a standing ovation.

Everett Case died four months later, on April 30, 1966, in a Raleigh hospital of complications from a bleeding intestine. He was eight weeks shy of his sixty-sixth birthday. More than six hundred people, including forty former players, were present at his funeral. Shortly before he died, he told a reporter that two games ranked in his memory as the top Wolfpack victories he had experienced. One was a 1952 NCAA Regional win over Villanova. The other was their semifinal defeat of Cincinnati in the 1958 Dixie Classic, the most memorable staging of the most engaging holiday basketball tournament in history.

As a final statement of his devotion to Wolfpack basketball and his players, Case amended his will shortly before his death to state the following: His one surviving relative, sister Blanche James, would received $198,000 of his estate and the remaining $69,525 would be divided up among his former players and associates in shares that he painstakingly outlined in the document. Willis Casey, who handled most of the details of the Dixie Classic each year, got three shares of the money, as did players like Vic Bubas, Ronnie Shavlik, Vic Molodet, and Lou Pucillo. Others, like John Richter and Smedes York, got two shares, and still others were bequeathed one share or a half share. None of the players linked to the point-shaving incidents were mentioned in the will.

Case had discussed the distribution of his assets with one of the executors of the will, telling him that he considered the players' excellence on the court while at N. C. State and their contributions to society after they graduated. He told the executor that he wanted to honor the players because they were responsible for his reputation as a coach. "Basically, the formula consisted of what the boy had attained with his basketball skills, what he did for the college both in athletics and academics, and what he had made of himself after he left school," said an article in the News and Observer after Case's will was made public.

Despite his host of health problems, many who loved Everett Case were convinced that the coach's rapid deterioration was linked to his heartbreak over the point-shaving scheme and the Wolfpack players who were sucked into it. Charlie Bryant visited Case frequently and was one of the last people to talk with him before he died, and up to the end Case was still revisiting that Georgia Tech game and his role in igniting the investigation that eventually consumed the Dixie Classic.

"It broke his heart," Bryant said. "I don't think he ever got over it, because his life was almost one hundred percent basketball. He was just such a unique person and had such a tremendous love for the game of basketball. It just literally broke his heart."

Epilogue

As impossible as it seemed to the N. C. State faithful, Everett Case was gone, and one of his earliest Indiana recruits, Norm Sloan, took the helm in 1966 intent on recapturing former Wolfpack glory. The Dixie Classic was becoming a memory, too, as the players who made it great moved on to life after college and even hoops-crazy legislators abandoned the idea of bringing back a masterpiece in the absence of its artist. But in the spirit of that tournament, in 1970 the coaches of the former Classic regulars started a new tradition in a new location—the Big Four Tournament in Greensboro, North Carolina.

The Big Four Tournament was designed to fill the void left by the Dixie Classic, and it featured N. C. State, North Carolina, Wake Forest, and Duke playing each other in a round-robin format in the Greensboro Coliseum, but it was still a shadow of its predecessor. It was staged in early December instead of enlivening the week after Christmas, and the field consisted of the Big Four only. Without visiting teams to beat up on, the Big Four coaches eventually soured on the idea of potentially amassing three conference losses that early in the season. The Big Four Tournament was ended after a decade with little fanfare.

Through the birth and death of that event and countless other tournaments that have featured Big Four teams, fondness for the Dixie Classic never abated. And fifty years after Everett Case's dream tournament met its end, the debate about the true cause of its demise raged on as well.

There is no confusion over the negotiations that took place between players like Don Gallagher and Stan Niewierowski and the gambling kingpins eager for a bigger windfall. Fans from all four schools agree that the point-fixing scheme did occur and that it was harmful to the game of basketball. But even though Bill Friday read an extensive statement detailing his belief that the fixes necessitated the end of the Dixie Classic, there still exists a contingency of people who disagree with his decision. Some understand his motives but think his reaction was overly harsh. Others believe that his actions that spring were rooted in loyalty to one university's team or resentment of another.

Bucky Waters distinguished himself early as a player for N. C. State and a head coach for West Virginia and Duke, but when he retired from coaching in 1973 he became famous as a prolific talker. In thirty years as a broadcaster, Waters covered almost every sport and was best-known as a college basketball analyst. So it should come as no surprise that he is quick to speak about the end of what he sees as the quintessential holiday tournament.

"Nobody respects Bill Friday more than I do," Waters said of the man who led public higher education in North Carolina for three decades. "He has been an icon for me. But when he cancelled the Dixie Classic he threw out the baby with the bathwater. A great, great tradition was sacrificed by what I call a knee jerk. And this is a guy who doesn't knee jerk. He's a giant."

As Waters sees it, dishonesty in college basketball goes back nearly as far as the sport itself. Gamblers had been conspiring with players for many years before the revelations of 1961, and he believes that it happened to a lesser extent even after the perpetrators were caught and punished. In recent years, game fixes engineered by gamblers have given way to payoffs orchestrated by agents and boosters. In both cases, the athlete cashes in on the promise of some quick money and finds himself beholden to powerful, connected people. Friday may have been sincere in his desire to stop such practices by cancelling the Dixie Classic, Waters said, but a quick glance at today's sports page shows the flood of corruption is still doing catastrophic damage to the college game.

"They came down hard on State and Carolina," Waters said. "I love Bill Friday. I really do. I just admire him so much, but I just cannot ever come to grips with what he did to the Dixie Classic. He squashed State and Carolina for two years, and his whole thing was to protect the kids or whatever, to bring college athletics back into proportion. The biggest negative is that the sacrifice that it made did not achieve any type of parity or cleanliness. It was just another chapter in the cycle of people hurting themselves and hurting other people."

Smedes York, a former N.C. State player under Everett Case who later became the mayor of Raleigh, has also never wavered in his belief that ending the Dixie Classic depleted a mother lode of business profit and fan fervor that has never been replenished by another sporting event. "Over the years my perspective has not changed," York said. "I felt like the Dixie Classic should not have been cancelled. It was a wonderful thing for the fans. People loved it. You need to have a strong discipline on what student-athletes are doing. That's very important, but I felt like that was too strong a measure. It didn't punish the right people."

Waters and York represent one category of dissenters to the Classic's cancellation: Those who trusted Friday's purpose but thought his chosen penalty exceeded the crime. But another group of Dixie Classic adherents believes that the tournament was actually called off because of resentment from influential UNC, Wake, or Duke boosters who thought Everett Case had built a shrine to N.C. State's tournament domination. Case designed the coliseum, selected the field, hired the officials, and used the spectacle as a magnetic draw for recruits. It was no secret that Frank McGuire and other coaches were getting a little tired of being perennial guests at Everett's big ball.

"Everett Case controlled the tickets," said Jack Murdock, who played for Wake Forest in the fifties and later coached there. "He also picked the referees. And the one big thing was that he could recruit on his own campus. Nobody else could. And I really think that had something to do with the opinion of some other coaches about the Classic. To bring in recruits and watch that spectacle was a heck of a deal. I don't begrudge Everett Case. If Everett Case had not come out of the military to coach here, I don't think this would be like it is today."

Vic Molodet was one of the best guards ever to play for N. C. State, and he has always believed that inter-university politics played a role in Friday's decision. Friday attended N. C. State as an undergrad, but he went to UNC for law school and kept his office on the Chapel Hill campus as the system president. To Molodet and some other Wolfpack faithful, it seemed feasible that influential UNC fans wanted to see the Dixie Classic disappear and lobbied Friday to make it happen.

"I don't like to mention names, but we all figured it was the head of the blue organization," said Molodet, referring to Tar Heels head coach Frank McGuire. "We had something there that no one else had. We made good money. We had tremendous crowds. But it was good for everybody. It was good for all four of the teams."

In early 2011, shortly after his ninetieth birthday, Bill Friday sat in his Chapel Hill office and considered the complaints of those who questioned his leadership during that difficult time in 1961. On that very day, new allegations against UNC football players had come out, widening the net of a scandal that implicated agents, tutors, and athletes and even led to the firing of head coach Butch Davis. The relationship between intercollegiate athletics and the academic institutions they represent was still a discouraging quagmire in 2011. But Friday's intentions that day were to maintain the integrity of the universities by keeping athletics in perspective, he said. And a half century later, he continues to beat that drum every time he gets a chance.

"That never entered my mind," Friday said when told that some believed he was bowing to the frustration of anti-N. C. State forces. "The thing that I was really worried about was the possibility of harm to these young men. That's why we did it. It was the right thing to do, because it was the only thing that we had an option to do.

"The Dixie Classic, in a way, was a forerunner of what's going on in American sports today. The NCAA is getting more serious about their sanctions. But the tragedy of it is that we have to do it at all, because we aren't here to run an entertainment business, we're here to run a good university. I'm all for sports. But I am not for this."

To Friday, potholes like that 2010 UNC football scandal or allegations of academic cheating in N. C. State basketball in the eighties only demonstrate the need for more vigilance. And at an age when most people are pursuing a life of retirement leisure, he has made a second career out of crusading for more accountability in college sports. In 1984, he was instrumental in passing Proposition 48, which established a minimum SAT score for all collegiate athletes.

In the late 1980s, with retired Notre Dame president Father Theodore Hesburgh, Friday helped organize a group called the Knight Commission to look into ways to stem the tide of excess in athletics. After several years of studying the problem, in 1991 the Knight Commission released a highly publicized report that called for a paradigm shift: An athlete in college would henceforth be known first as a student—with academic oversight taking precedence over athletic priorities—and second as an athlete. Still, the excesses continue, and Friday continues to put forth the same message that has always driven him.

"The sad thing about the picture you see today is that it's not only bigger, but it's worse," Friday said. "There's so much more money involved. We've turned the universities into entertainment centers. I'm not hollering, 'I told you so.' My answer to it all is, 'I'm very sad.' Because it's creating an aura around an institution that is deeply revered that ought never have happened. And the strong voices have got to rise up and say, 'No more of this. No. More. Of. This.' And maybe it will start to right itself.'"

To visit with Bill Friday is to be reminded of what's wrong with college sports. It's an echo of early 1961, when a new young hero was falling to earth every day in shattering headlines about point-shaving and a gem of a tournament called the Dixie Classic was never seen again. But to talk to George Blaney is to recapture the simple joy and influence of basketball that once captivated a legendary coach named Everett Case.

Blaney played in the 1959 Dixie Classic as a sharpshooting guard for the Holy Cross Crusaders. He then spent one season in the NBA before finding what would become his life's calling—coaching college basketball. When he helped guide the Connecticut Huskies to the 2011 national title as the associate head coach, he was finishing his forty-fourth consecutive season coaching at the collegiate level. The game and the athletes have changed since he first ran into Reynolds Coliseum to the strains of that Hammond organ, but after four decades Blaney still coaches for the same reason—because he believes in the power of basketball to shape young players into men.

"Great things have come out of the game, that's what's kept me in it for so long," Blaney said. "Through that you are able to influence kids' lives. The individuals who have not respected the game, they're in the minority. What's so great about the game is its ability to help so many people."

Dave Odom has spent a lifetime in college basketball as well, first as a coach and now as an organizer of a tournament that could be considered today's answer to the Dixie Classic, the exotic Maui Invitational. Like Everett Case did for the Dixie Classic, Odom invites teams to Maui in hopes of assembling a highly competitive field. But even though the basketball is intense in Maui, Odom's event, played in a small gym thousands of miles away from most of the team's fan bases, is the epitome of a made-for-TV tournament. The arena in Hawaii isn't packed with boys clutching precious ticket stubs and happily marinating in three days of top-notch basketball. Once one of those boys himself, at times Odom still pines for the spirited, smoky mayhem that was the Dixie Classic.

"It was the greatest three days," Odom said. "You saw four games a day and you saw the best teams in the country, the best players in the country, and the best coaches in the country, playing before the best fans in the country. It was easily the most respected and longed-for holiday tournament in the country, even to this day."

Acknowledgments

This book was born out of a favor from a friend, when Mike Stroud—a true N.C. State fan if there ever was one—agreed to drive his truck a couple of towns over to pick up a piece of used furniture I had purchased. As we drove, I told Mike that I was searching for a jewel of a story from North Carolina sports history—a tale that was just begging to be dusted off and told. He said, "How about the Dixie Classic?" and my new quest was defined.

Soon I was approaching men in their seventies and eighties, former players and perennial fans, and telling them that I wanted to talk about the Dixie Classic. The light in their eyes and their passion as memories flowed were abundant proof that I had chosen the right topic.

I interviewed fifty-five people who had a connection to the Classic, and without exception they were gracious and generous with their recollections. But one former N.C. State All-American, Lou Pucillo, took a special interest in the book and stepped in time and again with a phone number, a lead, or some timely encouragement. Lou was truly my ears on the ground in Raleigh, and this book would be considerably leaner without his contributions.

Tim Peeler, N.C. State's resident sports historian and a fellow writer, came to my aid in numerous ways, from reading manuscripts to unearthing precious Dixie Classic programs to searching down phone numbers. He supported this project from its inception and was patient with my seemingly endless flood of Wolfpack questions.

Many others from the Wolfpack Nation and the city of Raleigh agreed to talk about the tournament, and I am grateful to them: Alta Chalmers, Beverly Shavlik, Les Robinson, Charlie Bryant, Harry Stewart, Roman Gabriel, Ken Nye, Joe Harand, Governor Jim Hunt, Johnny Ballantine, Bill Hensley, C. A. Dillon, Vic Molodet, Larry Monteith, Speck Underwood, Smedes York, Bucky Waters, Vic Molodet, A. J. Carr, Frank Weedon, and Tim Nicholls, whose unforgettable Dixie Classic story serves as this book's opener.

Of course, the Classic was a stage set for all the Big Four, and players and coaches from every Tobacco Road school proved invaluable to this process. From Duke, I am thankful to Dick Groat, Richard Crowder, and Vic Bubas, who of course belongs to N. C. State as well. From North Carolina, the story came together with the help of Doug Moe, Charlie Thorne, Bob Young, Joel Fleishman, Bill Friday, Woody Durham, Pete Brennan, and Lennie Rosenbluth. And contributing memories from Wake Forest were Murray Greason, Jr., Alley Hart, Billy Packer, Dave Odom, Maurice George, Dickie Hemric, Jack Murdock, and gracious queen Connie Pinyoun Gamble.

The strands of this story led me to people all over North Carolina and across the United States, and those whose tales added value to the book include George Blaney, Joe Vancisin, Johnny Green, Tom Rand, Ernie Beck, Wayne Duke, Dick Frank, Dorsey Tyndall, George Whitfield, Wilbur Shirley, Irwin Smallwood, Joe Aufderheide, and Bill Cowan.

I also called on sports information staffs at Oregon, Michigan State, Pennsylvania, Villanova, and Seton Hall to help fill holes in my research, and all were quick to comb archives for me even when today's sporting events were certainly more pressing for them.

This decades-old story couldn't be pieced together from interviews alone, so I turned to numerous books to help paint the picture. Many of these books were valuable to me, but only one—*ACC Basketball: An Illustrated History*—was truly indispensable. Special thanks to Ron Morris for meticulous research and excellent storytelling.

This is not an East Carolina book per se, but my local university proved to be a wealth of research and writing assistance. I am especially grateful to ECU's Joyner Library, where I sat and wrote two or more days a week and made reams of copies upstairs on the microfilm machine in the Special Collections room. Thanks also to my friend John Ridley with the Baptist Campus Ministry, who graciously offered me a free place to park near the library.

I am fortunate enough to have a circle of friends that includes people of many talents, and I hit the jackpot when Stephanie Whitlock Dicken, a gifted graphic artist, agreed to design the cover. Among those patiently reading hundreds of pages of manuscripts—and improving the book considerably in the process—were Lisa Stroud and Nancy Gray, respectively a high school English teacher and a college journalism professor in their day jobs.

Countless friends contributed to this project in big and small ways with words of encouragement, thoughtful questions, offers to watch my kids, or the gift of quiet places to work. The framework of this book came together at a lovely quiet retreat on Bath Creek, courtesy of Rusty and Patsy Duke. Laura Von Gunten, Nicole Nelson, Leah Wilson, and Emily Baumgartner were generous with The Castle for a couple of productive writing days. And Laura Swayne, Sara Jennings, and Deanne Trollinger extended warm hospitality to me on interviewing trips throughout the state.

Kit Sublett, my long-suffering editor and publisher, persevered through meticulous editing sessions to the point of exhaustion and made himself into a college basketball expert by necessity. Our collaboration, and the years of friendship that preceded it, have indeed made the book better.

Finally, my family has doled out love and grace time and again, even when I was too preoccupied by book details to give it back in the measure they deserved. They have been my chief cheerleaders since day one; you haven't lived until you've picked your kids up in the carpool line and they've asked, "How many words did you write today, Mom?" Preston, Holly, Benjamin, and Jake: Thank you for being such great kids, always quick with a hug or a way to make me laugh. And to my husband Sid, who encouraged endlessly, read manuscripts faithfully, and listened to me process the story even when it surely became tiresome, I love you and can't imagine undertaking this adventure without you alongside.

Appendix: Results

1949
Champion: North Carolina State
MVP: Dick Dickey, North Carolina State
    First round:
        NCSU 81, Rhode Island State 64
        Penn State 51, Duke 48
        Georgia Tech 64, WFU 57
        West Virginia 58, Carolina 50
    Second round:
        Rhode Island State 61, WFU 57
        Carolina 59, Duke 52
        NCSU 57, Georgia Tech 34
        Penn State 46, West Virginia 41
    Final round:
        NCSU 50, Penn State 40
        Rhode Island State 65, Carolina 60
        Duke 54, WFU 52
        Georgia Tech 63, West Virginia 48

1950
Champion: North Carolina State
MVP: Sammy Ranzino, North Carolina State
    First round:
        Navy 60, Carolina 49
        NCSU 89, Tulane 75
        WFU 57, Rhode Island State 53
        Colgate 84, Duke 69
    Second round:
        NCSU 72, WFU 56
        Duke 71, Carolina 63
        Colgate 63, Navy 59
        Tulane 81, Rhode Island State 62
    Final round:
        NCSU 85, Colgate 76
        Duke 74, Tulane 72
        Rhode Island State 93, Carolina 69
        Navy 66, WFU 46

1951

Champion: North Carolina State
MVP: Lee Terrill, North Carolina State
    First round:
        Columbia 66, Duke 58
        Carolina 49, Southern California 45
        NCSU 71, Navy 51
        Cornell 58, WFU 51
    Second round:
        Cornell 66, Columbia 64
        NCSU 58, Carolina 51
        Southern California 80, Navy 64
        Duke 79, WFU 74
    Final round:
        NCSU 51, Cornell 49
        Carolina 61, Columbia 60
        Southern California 87, Duke 69
        Navy 79, Wake 44

1952

Champion: North Carolina State
MVP: Ernie Beck, Pennsylvania
    First round:
        Wake 65, Penn State 61
        Holy Cross 85, Carolina 73
        Brigham Young 69, Duke 68
        NCSU 87, Princeton 63
    Second round:
        NCSU 76, Holy Cross 74
        Brigham Young 84, WFU 58
        Carolina 73, Princeton 59
        Penn State 97, Duke 80
    Final round:
        NCSU 75, Brigham Young 59
        WFU 91, Holy Cross 69
        Penn State 70, Carolina 62
        Duke 75, Princeton 59

1953
Champion: Duke
MVP: Rudy D'Emilio, Duke
First round:
NCSU 72, Seton Hall 70
WFU 72, Tulane 65
Navy 86, Carolina 62
Duke 71, Oregon State 61
Second round:
Navy 85, NCSU 75
Duke 83, WFU 6
Seton Hall 73, Carolina 63
Tulane 74, Oregon State 70
Final round:
Duke 98, Navy 83
WFU 86, NCSU 79
Seton Hall 77, Tulane 68
Oregon State 65, Carolina 53

1954
Champion: North Carolina State
MVP: Ronnie Shavlik, North Carolina State
First round:
Carolina 67, Southern California 58
Minnesota 81, WFU 73
NCSU 95, Cornell 61
Duke 92, West Virginia 79
Second round:
Minnesota 79, Duke 73
NCSU 47, Carolina 44
WFU 96, West Virginia 94
Southern California 77, Cornell 58
Final round:
NCSU 85, Minnesota 84
Carolina 65, Duke 62
WFU 93, Southern California 85
West Virginia 79, Cornell 71

1955
Champion: North Carolina State
MVP: Ronnie Shavlik, North Carolina State
First round:
    NCSU 59, Oregon State 54
    WFU 87, Minnesota 83
    Duke 71, Wyoming 54
    Carolina 86, Villanova 63
Second round:
    NCSU 70, WFU 58
    Carolina 74, Duke 64
    Minnesota 64, Oregon State 60
    Wyoming 69, Villanova 68
Final round:
    NCSU 82, Carolina 60
    Duke 64, WFU 52
    Villanova 68, Oregon State 63
    Minnesota 70, Wyoming 66

1956
Champion: North Carolina
MVP: Lennie Rosenbluth, North Carolina
First round:
    WFU 74, DePaul 68
    Carolina 97, Utah 76
    NCSU 84, Iowa 70
    Duke 73 , West Virginia 67
Second round:
    Utah 83, West Virginia 66
    WFU 73, NCSU 66
    Carolina 87, Duke 71
    DePaul 73, Iowa 72
Final round:
    Carolina 63, WFU 55
    NCSU 102, Duke 80
    Utah 86, DePaul 79
    Iowa 79, West Virginia 76

1957

Champion: North Carolina
MVP: Pete Brennan, North Carolina

First round:

NCSU 71, Northwestern 68
WFU 64, Duquesne 54
Carolina 63, St. Louis 48
Duke 69, Seton Hall 62

Second round:

NCSU 63, WFU 61
Carolina 76, Duke 62
Northwestern 80, Duquesne 70
St. Louis 77, Seton Hall 44

Final round:

Carolina 39, NCSU 30
Duke 79, WFU 75 OT
Northwestern 66, St. Louis 53
Duquesne 68, Seton Hall 65

1958

Champion: North Carolina State
MVP: John Richter, North Carolina State

First round:

NCSU 67, Louisville 61
Cincinnati 94, WFU 70
Michigan State 82, Duke 57
Carolina 92, Yale 65

Second round:

NCSU 69, Cincinnati 60
Michigan State 75, Carolina 58
Louisville 74, WFU 64
Duke 56, Yale 53

Final round:

NCSU 70, Michigan State 61
Duke 57, Louisville 54
Carolina 90, Cincinnati 88
WFU 85, Yale 76

1959
Champion: Wake Forest
MVP: Billy Packer, Wake Forest
    First round:
        Dayton 36, NCSU 32
        WFU 80, Holy Cross 71
        Duke 63, Utah 52
        Carolina 72, Minnesota 65
    Second round:
        WFU 61, Dayton 50
        Carolina 75, Duke 55
        Holy Cross 63, NCSU 61
        Utah 75, Minnesota 72
    Final round:
        WFU 53, Carolina 50
        Dayton 71, Duke 63
        Utah 92, Holy Cross 84
        NCSU 57, Minnesota 48

1960
Champion: North Carolina
MVP: Doug Moe, North Carolina
    First round:
        Villanova 72, NCSU 63
        Carolina 81, Maryland 57
        Marquette 91, WFU 83
        Duke 86, Wyoming 59
    Second round:
        Carolina 87, Villanova 67
        Duke 86, Marquette 73
        NCSU 75, Maryland 67
        WFU 87, Wyoming 66
    Final round:
        Carolina 76, Duke 71
        Villanova 75, Marquette 70
        NCSU 99, WFU 91
        Maryland 84, Wyoming 77

Bibliography

Barrier, Smith. *On Tobacco Road: Basketball in North Carolina*. New York, New York: Leisure Press, 1983.

Chappelow, Craig. *Raleigh's Reynolds Coliseum*. Mount Pleasant, South Carolina: Arcadia Publishing, 2002.

Cohen, Stanley. *The Game They Played*. New York, New York: McGraw-Hill Ryerson Ltd., 1977.

Fox, Larry. *Illustrated History of Basketball*. New York, New York: Grosset & Dunlap, 1974.

Grundy, Pamela. *Learning to Win: Sports, Education, and Social Change in Twentieth-Century North Carolina*. Chapel Hill, North Carolina: The University of North Carolina Press, 2001.

Jacobs, Barry. *Across the Line: Profiles in Basketball Courage: Tales of the First Black Players in the ACC and SEC*. Guilford, Connecticut: The Lyons Press, 2008.

Jarrett, William S. *Timetables of Sports History: Basketball*. New York, New York: Facts on File, 1990.

McKinney, Bones, and Garland Atkins. *Bones: Honk your Horn if You Love Basketball*. North Carolina: Garland Publications, 1988.

Menzer, Joe. *Four Corners: How UNC, N.C. State, Duke and Wake Forest Made North Carolina the Center of the Basketball Universe*. New York, New York: Simon and Schuster, 1999.

Morris, Ron. *ACC Basketball: An Illustrated History*. Village Sports, 1988.

Powell, Adam. *University of North Carolina Basketball*. Mount Pleasant, South Carolina: Arcadia Publishing, 2005.

Robertson, Oscar. *The Big O: My Life, My Times, My Game.* Lincoln, Nebraska: University of Nebraska Press, 2003.

Rosen, Charley. *The Wizard of Odds: How Jack Molinas Almost Destroyed the Game of Basketball.* New York, New York: Seven Stories Press, 2002.

Shaw, Bynum. *The History of Wake Forest College, Volume IV.* Winston-Salem, North Carolina: Wake Forest University, 1988.

Index

Colophon

DESIGN

Art directed by Randolph McMann for Whitecaps Media

Cover designed by Stephanie Whitlock Dicken (cover photos courtesy of The North Carolina State Archives)

Main body composed in Charter ITC, a font by Matthew Carter. Chapter titles composed in Swing

PHOTO CREDITS

Unless otherwise noted, all photographs appear courtesy of The North Carolina State Archives

Courtesy of UNC Athletic Communications: photo of Frank McGuire holding basketball and photo of the UNC team celebrating their 1957 victory

Courtesy of Wake Forest Athletic Communications: photo of Bones McKinney on the sidelines and photo of Murray Greason with two players

Courtesy of North Carolina Collection, University of North Carolina Library at Chapel Hill: photo of William Friday

Courtesy of Les Robinson: Everett Case's Christmas card

Jacket illustration of Bethany Bradsher by Katy Biagini

About the Author

BETHANY BRADSHER has been covering North Carolina athletics for the past sixteen years and has been a journalist since 1990. She is the author of *Coaching Third: The Keith LeClair Story*, which was published by Whitecaps Media in 2010.

In 1995 as a sportswriter for the Spartanburg *Herald-Journal*, she covered the inaugural two seasons of the Carolina Panthers and the preparations for the 1996 Summer Olympics in Atlanta. She has written for the Associated Press, the Durham *Herald-Sun*, the Orlando *Sentinel*, and the Houston *Post*, as well as many magazines.

She and her husband Sid live in Greenville, North Carolina, with their four children.